BILL SIMS JR.

green beans & ice cream

THE REMARKABLE POWER OF POSITIVE REINFORCEMENT

ORDER YOUR BOOK TODAY AT WWW.GREENBEANBOOK.COM

"It must be realized that there is nothing more difficult to plan, more uncertain of success, or more dangerous to manage than a new order of things . . . for he who introduces it makes enemies of all those who derived advantage from the old order and finds but lukewarm defenders among those who stand to gain from the new one.

Such a lukewarm attitude grows partly out of fear of the adversaries and partly from the incredulity of men in general, who actually have no faith in new things until they have been proven by experience."

—Niccolo Machiavelli, circa 1513

Table of Contents

1. **R+** is a registered trademark of Aubrey Daniels International, Inc. Used with permission.

1. **R+** is a registered trademark of Aubrey Daniels International, Inc. Used with permission.

Foreword...

Well here it is—my first book. This was a lot harder than I thought it would be... I hope you enjoy it. You are holding the culmination of my life's work (nearly 30 years) in the area of positive reinforcement and employee motivation/behavior change at large and small North American firms.

In the movie that bears his name, Forrest Gump said, "Life is like a box of chocolates." I think my life has proven him to be correct. My early years in business can best be summed up as the proverbial "start-up with a shoe-string budget," "wing and a prayer," and "the school of hard knocks." Many years later, when I started talking about Green Beans and Ice Cream, I had no idea that people around the world would want to hear the message, and that it would resonate so strongly with them. I am humbled that it has touched so many hearts and hope that in some small way it will make a difference for you too.

While there is a long, long list of people who have inspired and helped me, I respect your patience as my reader and readily acknowledge that we cannot list them all. Nevertheless, just a few of those I wish to thank from my professional world are Aubrey Daniels, Bob Nelson, Gene Owens, Gail Snyder, George Self, Mark and Neil Biteler, Doug Hamilton, Dave Stanley, Vic Anapolle, Ray Miller, Bruce Majors, Diana Linville, Ken Yockey,

Larry Beggs, Kenny Sawyer, Barbara Glanz, Leo Inghilleri, Billy Yarbrough, Max Dover, Lisa Kane, Bob Coleman, Jane Greer, Keith Johanson, Marie Jones, Bob Veazie, Jitu Patel, Faiz Al-Thiga, Ann Lindsey, Tom Hippe, Ron Ellis, Darryl Oscars, Tommy Sides, Rudi Fillingim, Mike Gibney, and Steve Kopecki—I thank all of you for believing in me and for the different perspectives on human behavior that you have helped me to see.

From the bottom of my heart, I thank my mother Edna, and my father Bill Sr., for being the two parents that every kid wants to have, and for patiently guiding and mentoring me. I honor my brother David and sister Bonnie for their hard work alongside me. I thank my wife Margie for believing in me when the chips were down. Finally I both commend and thank my two precious daughters, Carli and Daphne, for making our home a cherished place to return to after all those long, hard days, and for letting your daddy get on yet another airplane. I love you all...b ☺

ONE
The Little Rebel

It was suppertime, and there they were again:

Green.

Slimy.

Stringy.

My worst nightmare—yeah, it was green beans all right—again.

By the time I was a four-year-old kid, I had already sampled green beans and concluded they weren't for me. The strings might as well have been wood chips, the way they caught in my throat as I tried to get them down.

Mom was my boss, and I was her newest employee. We had a real labor/management crisis going on. She begged, cajoled, and pleaded. But I was determined not to eat those green beans.

So I crossed my arms, frowned, and pouted, figuring she'd give up and forget about green beans, as she always had in the past.

But this time, Mom had a secret weapon. Now, there was something else on the table besides that dreaded green scourge.

"Billy Joe, if you eat your green beans you can have some..."

You guessed it.

"Ice cream!"

This sheer stroke of maternal genius changed my behavior forever. In a flash, I saw those green beans, not as an oppressive burden, but as a first-class ticket to that lovely ice cream.

Sure, Mom got what she wanted—a balanced diet for her four-year-old.

And I got ice cream.

Pretty cool.

(Thanks, Mom. You are the best!)

I'm not sure exactly when or how Mom pared back the ice cream, but somehow I came to terms with green beans and accepted them for what they are—pretty healthy and tasty by themselves (oh, Mom learned to buy stringless beans, and that didn't hurt either).

Mom had learned how to change my behavior!

TWO

Why Did He Do That?

Understanding why people do what they do is one of our most daunting challenges. Human behavior has been a subject of discussion since man emerged from the dust.

Understanding behavior is a formidable challenge, but it also offers us huge rewards—if we can only crack the code of human behavior *change*.

Consider a few examples of the power of human behavior:

- Hitler's focusing the genius of a respected nation on the execution of evil.
- The decision to drop the atomic bomb on Japan, an event that brought a proud, powerful country to its knees and dominated international relations for generations to come.

- The 9-11-2001 attack on the World Trade Center and the Pentagon.
- The 1999 massacre at Columbine High School in Colorado.
- Going "Postal"—a phenomenon named for the series of violent and lethal outbursts by disgruntled U.S. Postal Service employees during the 1980s and 1990s.

All of these events included a common factor: human behavior that shaped the world as we know it. After all, what is a country, a family, a school, a business? While the environment, buildings, equipment, and furniture are certainly important, it is the tapestry of human behavior that creates what we call "culture".

Culture is made up of many small behaviors and activities. Sometimes we say that the culture is "toxic" or "nurturing". Many people assume that culture is what it is, and can never be changed. At best, they will say that culture change requires a long time.

I beg to differ. Ask Hosni Mubarak (Egypt's strongman before the Arab Spring melted his power base) how fast culture can change.

Consider the sudden, unexpected collapse of the Soviet Union and the dismantling of the Berlin Wall.

Consider this common scenario in the business world:

A president unveils his new plan to turn around his failing company.

"It won't work, sir," comes the timid response from his staff.

"And why not?"

"The culture here won't support it."

"*Culture*! What's that? A fuzzy word to hide a lame excuse!" retorts the frustrated leader.

Sure enough, his plan fails, torpedoed by culture.

The word *culture* is often hard to define. Here's a definition I like: "Culture is a pattern of behavior which is encouraged or punished by the management system over time."

In reality then, to change culture, all we have to do is change behavior. Attitudes follow behavior, just as my attitude about green beans changed over time, after my behavior changed.

But many have been misinformed. An old friend of mine, whom I'd not seen for 20 years, learned about my work in behavior change. In a telephone conversation, he offered up his two cents worth on the subject: "Bill, I remember my professor in psychology to this day. He told me that before you can change behavior, you have to change attitude."

I swallowed hard. He was a good friend, and it had been a long time since we'd talked to each other.

"Crad," I told him, "I hope you won't be upset, but when I see you, I'd really appreciate it if you'd let me tell you why your professor was wrong."

I guess he still likes me, because we went to lunch soon afterward, and I was able to explain to him that to change attitude, you simply have to change behavior. He even asked me to present to a group of 200 company leaders on the subject of positive reinforcement and behavior change!

No matter whether you are a parent, husband, wife, teacher, boss, supervisor, professor, cop, or anything else in life, what you often want from the people around you is the same thing: behavior change.

You want more production, quality, safety, and customer service from your employees; better test scores, homework, and study habits from your students; cleaner rooms and better grades from your kids. To get more from people, we need behavior change.

Everything we observe can be broken down into behaviors, activities, results, and culture. If culture is Beethoven's Fifth Symphony, then every note from every instrument can be likened to a behavior.

Results are achieved by a myriad of behaviors. Think of your favorite dessert. That dessert is the result. But the sugar, flour, butter and other items that make up the dessert are behaviors. When we get the behaviors right, we can cook up some amazing results!

Culture, like a dessert, can be toxic or nurturing. There's nothing like luscious banana pudding to add warmth and flavor to a meal. But a notorious husband-killer in North Carolina—known as the Black Widow—used banana pudding laced with arsenic to do away with her spouses.

So how do we achieve that nurturing culture?

Can we really navigate the murky world of the human mind? B. F. Skinner, American behaviorist, social philosopher, and poet, once wrote, "Thoughts are behaviors we haven't learned to observe yet."

Until technology allows it, you can't see inside my mind, and I can't see inside yours either. This "black hole" of human logic means that if we believe attitude must change before behavior, then we will be waiting a very, very long time to see any measurable difference in human performance. Just ask the Marlboro man how many years he read the Surgeon General's warning printed on every pack of cigarettes he smoked. Did those produce behavior change in him? It was not until he was in the hospital, terminally ill with cancer, that his attitude about smoking finally changed. Powerful consequences had forever changed his life, his behavior, and finally, his attitude toward smoking.

Since the complex world of human thought and attitude is at present not easily read, we need another tool to understand human behavior, one that we can implement easily in today's business world.

That tool has existed for more than 70 years. It's a science called "behavioral analysis".

Using some simple and easy tools, we can crack the code that reveals why people do what they do. And we can empower ourselves and others to achieve performance we never thought possible.

This book is devoted to helping you do just that . . .

THREE

Changing Attitudes and Self-Motivation

Applause bursts out spontaneously from a crowd delighted by the band's performance.

A coach shares a high-five with the player who wins the game.

A baby's first steps are applauded by Mom and Dad.

As hard as Alfie Kohn, Daniel Pink, and others may try to persuade us that external praise and positive feedback are wrong, their arguments do not jibe with the reality of life.

We need positive reinforcement. We cherish feedback confirming that our contributions matter and that we have made a difference in the world around us. Aubrey Daniels has coined a great name for this: R+®. From now on in this book, when you see the abbreviation "R+," you'll know that I am referring to positive reinforcement (of behavior), the most powerful tool on the planet for increasing human performance.

BUTTERFLY KISSES

"I know the cake looks funny, Daddy, but I sure tried." In this short line from "Butterfly Kisses", a song written by Bob Carlisle and Randy Thomas, a little girl reaches out for her father's approval (positive feedback) to be sure he sees her effort, and he appreciates it.

Bob Nelson's book, *1001 Ways to Reward Your Employees,* reports that of the key drivers of employee happiness and engagement, a recurring top need was "I am able to make a difference at work" and "My manager has recognized me recently for what I do."

Like the little girl in "Butterfly Kisses", people need to receive feedback from their leaders confirming that their work has value, and they are keenly aware of the presence of this feedback, or the lack thereof.

As we pass through a murky, chaotic, ever-changing world, we are anchored by that first "A" from our teacher; that first "Good Citizen" award certificate; that first knowledge that we came, we saw, and we made a positive difference.

Self-reinforcement is a very powerful form of R+ (assuming you aren't suffering from depression).

As my good friend Leo Inghilleri—a highly regarded consultant in the service and hospitality industry—once said, "The problem with highly self-motivated people is that they tend to assume everyone else is just like them."

Often, presidents and leaders of companies have very high levels of self-R+ around work ethic. When they are told that their employees need R+ to ensure that they continue to perform at their best, their response is often "But nobody did that for me, so why should I do it for others?"

So often they don't realize that someone did do this for them—a teacher, a parent, a mentor, who gave them positive reinforcement early on.

"When it's game time,
it's pain time, baby."
—TERRIBLE TERRY TATE,
Reebok Super Bowl
Commercial

FOUR

Does Punishment Really Work?

Does punishment really change behavior?

In an award-winning Super Bowl commercial, Reebok poked fun at "tough guy" management styles.

"When we asked Reebok to help us improve office productivity, we had no clue how effective their methods would be," says the CEO in the commercial.

Next we see employees goofing off on their jobs, only to be tackled, mauled and screamed at by Terrible Terry Tate, the big, bad football player: "When it's game time, it's pain time!"

"In fact, we wish Reebok had sent us ten Terry Tates," the smiling CEO says.

As funny as this clip is, it rings all too true for many of us.
Does punishment really work over the long haul?

Against his will, Terry Tate is finally sent on vacation, where
he spurs the lackluster hotel staff to unprecedented customer
service.

But while he is gone, what happens back at his home office?
Margaritaville parties and loss of performance.

While the cat's away, the mice will play. Terry returns to work,
realizing that behavior change lasts only as long as he is standing there holding the stick.

To watch the video, scan the QR Code below or visit
www.powerofpositivereinforcement.com

THE WASP AND THE HARD HAT

In London, four workers are building a brick wall, all wearing
their hard hats, as required. Out of nowhere, a wasp flies under
one man's hat. The worker quickly doffs the hat. Around the
corner comes his boss, who yells: "If you don't put your hard hat
on, you're off the project!"

Embarrassed, the red-faced worker puts his hard hat on, while
his buddies laugh at him. Convinced that his negative methods
have changed behavior, the boss marches off. The supervisor,
you see, has just received R+ for screaming at people (because
the worker put his hard hat on) and so he repeats the behavior
with renewed fervor.

Once the boss has gone, what does the worker do with his hard hat?

You guessed it. He takes it off.

What do we learn from this vignette?

Initially, the worker changed his behavior to avoid punishment from his boss.

The boss, therefore, is convinced that punishment and negative reinforcement "work", since the worker changed behavior. Negative reinforcement produces a temporary shift in behavior (just enough to avoid the pain), which is quickly followed by a reversion to a lower level of performance once the bully has gone.

Once the manager is gone, the worker shows who the real "boss" is when the hard hat comes back off.

Punishment and negative or "Leave Alone/Zap" managers get behavior change only when they are there holding the stick.

This same scenario plays out time after time in schools, workplaces—and in families.

"Set the table!"

The young girl grudgingly stops her homework assignment to set the table for dinner.

"Clean your room!"

With a sigh, she heads off to clean her room.

We often tend to use negative reinforcement because we believe it to be the most effective.

"Yes sir, Sir!"

But when we leave, what do people do?

Are the rooms really clean? Is the homework truly done? Are the hard hats on or off? Is the class quiet or rowdy?

One employee quit her job because: "When I make a mistake, my boss says something about it 100 percent of the time; when I work extra hard, he says nothing about it 99 percent of the time."

PEOPLE DON'T LEAVE COMPANIES; THEY LEAVE MANAGERS.

People don't leave a company; they leave their manager, as the study described below showed:

"Many workers feel stressed out, undervalued and dissatisfied with their job," according to a survey released March 8 by the American Psychological Association. Conducted online between Jan. 31 and Feb. 8, the survey found that 36 percent of the workforce experiences job stress regularly. Although nearly half of respondents cited low salary as having a significant impact on their stress levels, other factors commonly cited included lack of opportunities for advancement (43 percent), heavy workload (43 percent), unrealistic job expectations (40 percent) and long hours (39 percent). Slightly more than one-half of workers reported feeling valued on the job, while nearly one-third reported they intend to seek employment elsewhere in the coming year."

The only bone I have to pick with this survey is that the researchers did not include questions about the lack or presence of R+ in their assessment. It's safe to conclude that lack of R+ is the undercurrent "master problem" driving this employee disengagement.

An Australian CEO lamented to me that he had designed the perfect recognition solution, but none of his managers used it.

Sadly, he had never given anything but punishment and negative reinforcement to his direct reports, which like some other unpleasant things, tends to continue rolling downhill.

Does punishment change behavior?

Absolutely.

But the behavior change is short-lived and it fades as quickly as the punisher's dark shadow leaves the room. And managers who choose punishment as their tool of choice have only one option to change behavior—more severe levels of punishment (curt remarks, reprimands, yelling, written warnings, docking of pay, suspension, dismissal).

A classic example is the collection of internal memos written by the owner of Tiger Oil during the 1970s. The owner becomes increasingly insulting and demeaning to his workforce. You can see that he has lost all control, and so he resorts to louder and more frequent threats. Such memos today would prompt a string of lawsuits, but they were "part of the job" when I started my career in the late 1970s and early 1980s.

Read the memos at the QR Code below or visit
www.powerofpositivereinforcement.com
and click on "Diary of a Punisher".

Punishers get exactly what they intend as long as they are standing by to deliver more punishment; the problem is that they have no clue about all the performance—or non-performance—going on in their absence.

The bottom line: you can't *punish* a team into winning the Super Bowl.

Or, as Bob Nelson, best-selling author and motivational speaker, expressed it: "You get the best results by creating a fire within people, not by lighting a fire under them."

FIVE
The Church of Here and Now

To get an understanding of consequences and how they drive our behavior, consider the everyday light switch on a wall. When you flip up the switch, at least 99.9 percent of the time the lights will come on. That is an immediate consequence of flipping the switch.

Positive, immediate and certain consequences cause you and me to repeat that behavior again and again. We now flip light switches without even having to think about them. We are on "auto-pilot" for this behavior.

On the other hand, if you flip up a light switch and you get a nasty shock. . . then those negative and immediate consequences shut down or punish the behavior of flipping light switches. So, when it comes to behavior, people attend the Church of the Here and Now.

Behavioral science also focuses on punishment and penalty, which are all unpleasant. They too will shut down or decrease behavior. In this book, I am focusing on the unique power of positive reinforcement, which blows the doors off all the other kinds of consequences when it comes to attaining human performance improvement.

Volkswagen sponsored an intriguing study of how positive consequences alter human behavior.

To watch the video, scan the QR Code below or visit www.powerofpositivereinforcement.com and click the Piano Stairs link

SIX

Why Does R+ Work?

Donna was a new manager struggling to get her 300 highway-construction workers to comply with a new company safety rule: wearing a hard hat at all times. She'd done more than her share of yelling and screaming, trying to get compliance with the new rule.

Terry Tate would have been proud. Only nobody was taking her seriously.

"Why don't you try some R+?" I asked her. She agreed to give it a shot, and so I sent her my "R+ Care Package," which consisted of a big cooler chest that I felt sure any construction worker would appreciate.

The next day she showed up unexpectedly at a construction site. Following my suggestion, she singled out the only worker who was demonstrating the desired behavior.

Of the 17 guys on the project, only the newest employee was wearing a hard hat (apparently nobody had yet told him that wearing his hard hat was uncool).

Donna walked over to the new employee in front of everyone, while she ignored those who were not wearing their protective gear. She publicly thanked him (that was a little risky but it worked out well this time) for wearing his hard hat, telling him, "Joe, I really appreciate your taking safety seriously. I sometimes lie awake at night worried that one of you won't go home to your family safely, and your taking the time to follow our new safety rule means a lot to me. This gift is for you."

As the 16 rough, weathered construction workers watched, Donna presented the cooler chest to Joe. He responded, "Thanks, Donna! I've never won anything in my whole life, and nobody in safety has ever told me I did something right."

Now the 16 other construction workers asked Donna a question, "Where's our cooler chest?"

"Well guys, where are your hard hats? Maybe during my next safety audit, if I see you with your hard hats on, then we'll talk about cooler chests."

The impact on the other employees was immediate and powerful. On the next trip to the site, Donna was greeted by the entire crew smiling at her and pointing at their hard hats. Donna followed my advice and presented each one with a cooler chest and sincere positive feedback.

R+ works!

SEVEN

Blinded by the Light

It's 1927, and we're at the Hawthorne Works, a factory in Cicero, Illinois. A small group of women have been selected to participate in a unique study to see how lighting affects their productivity. The engineers doing the study are closely monitoring them. They want to see if dimming the lights will affect their productivity. The first week of the study, the researchers lower the lights by 10 percent, and they track the productivity of the team. Amazingly, production increases. The next week, they dim the lights again, and—voilà!—production increases. During the entire time, the workers receive feedback on the number of parts they are producing. This process goes on for a time, with the room getting ever darker and productivity going onward and upward, until it's so dark that the poor ladies can barely see.

The researchers decide to return the lights to full strength, expecting to erase their previous productivity gains, only to find that when the lights are returned to the original setting, *productivity increases again.*

The researchers reach an astounding conclusion: lighting has no effect on worker productivity.

What produced the effect? The fact that workers received feedback on their performance as well as autonomy in making work decisions (in later experiments the workers could vote on the length of the work day, the frequency and duration of breaks, and so on). All of this somehow produced what today is known as the "Hawthorne Effect".

EIGHT
Why Cash Isn't King

In his 1959 book, *The Motivation to Work,* Dr. Frederick Herzberg explained that the two greatest drivers of employee satisfaction are recognition and achievement, while money ranks a distant sixth place as a satisfier. Perhaps even more fascinating is that money did rank number one as a source of worker disengagement and unhappiness. Unfair pay erodes trust in leadership and decreases performance.

Then, in 1996, Bob Nelson conducted a number of surveys to discover that the most powerful driver of employee satisfaction and engagement isn't money; it's R+. Money again ranked a distant fifth place as a satisfier. Sadly, more than 68 percent of all workers have never heard the words "Thank you" from their bosses.

Nelson next interviewed the managers of those same employees to see what they believed would motivate their people. Money was their number-one response. Nearly all of those leaders felt that positive reinforcement and feedback would have little or no impact on worker behavior and performance.

The key takeaway from the Nelson study is that there is a huge disconnect between what workers say they want and what managers think they want. Managers see money as the answer, while workers say R+ is more important.

Perhaps what sums it up best is this story, reportedly told during an exit interview with a highly paid attorney, who quit her job to become a waitress. During the interview she was asked why she had chosen to take a pay cut of more than $100,000 per a year to become a waitress.

"I'll be honest," she said. "My boss says *something* 100 percent of the time when I make a mistake. And when I put forth extra effort, he says *nothing* 99 percent of the time. At least when I put the customer's breakfast on the table I'll get a 'Thank you.'"

Her manager's style is a classic. In my experience, more than 95 percent of leaders today are using that style without even being aware it has a name: Leave Alone/Zap management.

In his book, *The One Minute Manager*, Ken Blanchard coined the term "Leave Alone/Zap" to describe a management style in which supervisors leave the workers alone and say nothing when they are doing the job well, and then zap them when they make a mistake. Why do so many managers hesitate to use R+?

Perhaps the fear is that if we commend workers for work well done, it will encourage them to ask for pay raises (which is punishing for the managers).

In the book, *How Starbucks Saved My Life*, author Michael Gates Gill recounts a memo sent during the 1960s to all the managers of the J. Walter Thompson (JWT) ad agency. The memo ordered JWT managers: "Never positively recognize employees in writing, since they could use this against the company if they are fired."

Now, most managers think they do a great job at recognizing their employees and believe that a culture of R+ exists in their company.

"Come visit our company and you'll see, Bill! We just finished a week-long, employee-appreciation celebration. We took all the employees out for a full day at a local amusement park and bought them a nice dinner."

While I applaud the intention of this celebration, I can tell you without a doubt that such events do not drive better employee performance. In fact, they punish your outstanding workers, and reward your worst ones. (See Chapter 20: "Cave People: One Size Does Not Fit All.")

Another touching story concerns Norman the Doorman, who made a difference for me during a trip to the El Conquistador Resort in Puerto Rico.

To view that story, scan the QR Code below or visit
www.powerofpositivereinforcement.com

NINE
The
$3,000 Jacket

The Motor Convoy, a new-car hauler based in Decatur, Georgia, had offered $400 cash to every driver who completed a quarter with a perfect driving record, meaning no damages to the vehicles.

One day, I met with Biff Wilson, the company's vice president, to suggest a bold plan: "Biff, we can help you motivate these guys with a simple R+ solution that will give you better results at lower cost than your cash program."

One day, out of the blue, Biff gave me a call.

"Bill," he said, "We've decided to give you a chance at our business. We want to work with you on our next performance-improvement program."

I was delighted.

"What will the budget be?" I asked. Naively, I assumed it would be lower than the $400,000 in cash awards he'd been spending every quarter for the last few years, because I had promised to save him some money, but I was a bit surprised by his answer.

"I'm a little embarrassed to say this, Bill, but we were thinking more like $35,000," he told me. "Business has been kinda tough lately."

"Biff, let me be honest with you," I responded. "There's no way we can match the results of your $400,000 cash budget with a $35,000 R+ solution. I'm not sure I can help you."

However, after a lot of soul searching, I accepted Biff's "Mission Impossible" challenge, wondering what we could possibly offer for $35 that would have the impact of the $400 cash prize that the drivers had become accustomed to earning every three months.

During the early 1980s, the Member's Only jacket was a runaway best-seller. These jackets were hard to find, but they were really cool (at the time). They had a dog-leash collar and epaulets. Some of you may remember them. Together, Biff and I located a supplier who would provide us with enough jackets for every driver, and we had them embroidered with a special "Motor Convoy Professional Driver" emblem.

Biff and his leaders then explained to the drivers that the company was having some tough times, and while it hoped to re-institute the $400 cash bonus in the future, for this next go-round it wouldn't be possible.

"But we still want to honor our safe drivers by awarding this special jacket to those of you who can drive this quarter without damaging a vehicle," said Biff. "The jacket will never be repeated, so it should become a collector's item."

He went on to explain that for three months of error-free work, a driver would receive this jacket in lieu of the $400 cash. And that's how we began the three-month contest.

Those were the longest three months of my life.

At the end of the program, I called Biff. "How'd it go?"

"Bill, we've had better results from this R+ approach than from any of the cash awards before it."

"Wow! That's great, Biff."

I breathed a huge sigh of relief.

"Can you explain why R+ worked so well for you?" I asked.

Biff responded with a story:

"On the last day of the contest, we had a driver damage a vehicle. It was a pretty serious accident, and it caused over $3,000 in damage to a brand-new car. The employee drove more than four hours to see me. He sat in my office and asked if he could purchase the car, saying he would personally pay the more than $3,000 in repair costs."

"Why on Earth would you do that?" Biff asked him.

"Because I don't want to be the only guy in my terminal without a jacket."

I learned then and there about the power of R+.

Now the real question is this: "What did Biff Wilson do?"

Did he allow the worker to buy the car and receive the jacket?

Or did he tell the worker no, fearing it would cheapen the award for the other drivers? It was to be one of the most difficult decisions Biff had to make in his entire career as a leader.

At the end of the day, Biff elected *not* to give the worker a jacket, since it would cheapen the award for everyone else. Over 25 years later, I heard another story about jackets and worker behavior in Alaska that confirms Biff's decision.

To learn more about the Biff Wilson Alaska Jacket story,
scan the QR Code below or visit
www.powerofpositivereinforcement.com

"Human thoughts are
behaviors we have not yet
learned how to observe."
—B.F. SKINNER

TEN

Behaviors We Haven't Learned to Observe

Skinner made the statement above as a nod to the world of cognitive therapy. It rings true today, but my guess is that technology soon will allow us to begin observing thoughts as easily as we now observe physical behaviors.

As evidence, consider the Neuron Study. It proves undeniably the power of R+ and is an early attempt at measuring those elusive brain behaviors to which Skinner referred.

Figure 1
The Neuron Study

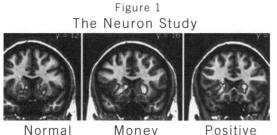

Normal   Money   Positive
                               Reinforcement

Strapped to an MRI, people were first given money, while having their brains scanned. Two very specific parts of the brain registered activity (see Figure 1). The section of the brain stimulated is a "pleasure center" called the striatum. It is stimulated not only by money but also by risky or unsafe behavior, such as pulling a slot machine lever.

Next, the Neuron researchers gave people commendation and R+.

You can see the result in the scan to the far right.

R+ causes the striatum areas to light up.

Wow!

The lesson: We do not have unlimited money to throw at people to motivate them and change their behavior. Eventually we run out of cash. But we never run out of R+. It is the most powerful tool for behavior change we have as leaders, and it is the tool that we use the least.

Even more interesting is that being thankful makes us happier too. A university study showed that people who were asked to dwell on positive thoughts about people who had helped them had far fewer illnesses than people who were asked to think of all the negative moments in their past.

ELEVEN

Why Do I Have to Recognize People Anyway?

Some people have the hardest time connecting R+ with behavior change.

But the evidence is all around us. Here is one of the favorite excuses people have for not recognizing people, and one of my myth-buster responses.

"Why do I have to R+ people? Isn't a paycheck enough?"

This objection is one of my favorites. When I conduct leadership training on R+, I often ask the leaders to vote as to whether or not a paycheck is positive reinforcement. Usually this question splits the audience down the middle, with half saying yes and the other half vehemently saying no.

At this point I usually turn to the senior leader in the room and point out that, in case nobody has noticed it, there is some pretty big disagreement as to what, exactly, R+ is and is not. If you can't agree on whether something as simple as a paycheck is R+, how can you hope to execute consistently on a strategy of delivering R+ as a team?

Until leaders can consistently agree on what R+ is, they will spin their wheels and fail hopelessly in their attempts to deploy it.

There are a few other things to ponder about paychecks. In today's workplace, there is usually less than a 3 percent differential in pay between underperforming employees and the highly motivated ones.

With these low stakes, it is foolish to expect people to sustain high-performance extra efforts based on money alone. R+ is the most cost-effective motivator we can use. In many cases, it's free.

TWELVE

"Stop Recognizing Those Employees!"

Why did this CEO take such extreme measures? His fears centered on the likelihood that managers might bestow their recognition on their friends instead of on the people who really deserved it. This is a valid concern, since management favoritism is a major source of employee disengagement.

The solution? Carefully pinpoint the desired behaviors and results you need, and positively reinforce them daily for everyone. Track the R+ to be sure it's used systematically to reach your organizational goals.

The devil is in the details. One day, Jan, a manager of a customer-service department called me in tears.

"I am about to quit my job, Bill!" Jan lamented. She explained why. Against her wishes, her CEO had installed recording systems to monitor the quality of calls into the Customer Service Department, which she managed. After a month or two, the CEO called her into his office.

"Your team isn't wowing the customer," he roared. "You need to do better!"

Jan asked him to pinpoint the behaviors he desired.

"I asked him what 'wowing' our customers would look like," she said.

She told him, "Sir, if you will tell me specifically what you want my team to do and say, we will do it. I promise that."

Apparently, the CEO knew what he wanted, but he didn't know how to get it. He never got back to Jan with any specifics. Jan quit her job a short time later.

THIRTEEN

A T-Shirt for a Million-Dollar Idea?

In the article, "How Hard Could It Be?" in the January 2009 issue of *Inc. Magazine*, Joel Spolsky struggled with the problem of how best to recognize a young employee's brilliant contribution to his bottom line. A young summer intern came up with an idea for a change to the company's website that generated more than $1 million a year in profits. [Hey, I'd hire that kid in a second.]

Joel, the CEO of Fogwire Software, struggled with a thorny question: "How do you properly compensate an employee for a smash-hit, million-dollar idea?"

He reasoned:

"On the one hand, you could argue [hold your applause please] that you don't have to compensate the employee; a software business is basically an idea factory." Joel rationalized that Fogwire was already paying Noah for his ideas. That was the nature of his employment agreement. Why pay twice?

"I felt we needed to do something else to express our gratitude," Joel wrote. "Should we buy Noah an Xbox 360? Pay him a bonus? Give him a T-shirt that said 'I Invented a Million-Dollar Business and All I Got Was This Lousy T-Shirt?' We were stumped."

Joel continued: "How do you pay employees based on performance when performance is so hard to quantify?"

The next few paragraphs of the Spolsky article absolutely fascinate me. I describe them as symptomatic of those who have been drinking too much "Pink Kool-Aid."

"Psychologists talk about two kinds of motivation: intrinsic and extrinsic," he wrote. "Intrinsic motivation is what drives you to do something regardless of whether you will receive a reward (I call it Self-R+). Extrinsic motivation is the drive to do something precisely because you expect to receive compensation, and it's the weaker of the two (I break Extrinsic into two sub-categories: External Social R+ and External Tangible R+)."

[Note: At this point it is obvious that Joel has been binging on Pink Kool-Aid. For more on this, read Chapter 29: "Don't Drink the Pink Kool-Aid".]

"Furthermore, the minute you start giving bonuses to reward performance, people start to compare themselves with their coworkers: *"Why didn't I get as much?"*

Joel solved his internal struggle with a stroke of genius: "So we decided to give Noah (our million-dollar idea employee) 10,000 shares of company stock—conditional on his coming back to work for us full-time when he graduated."

One small problem: the value of that stock is uncertain,

since Fogwire is a private enterprise, subject to fluctuations in the marketplace. Joel himself noted: "It wasn't a perfect solution, but everybody agreed that it made sense."

Joel added that when the award was presented Noah seemed pleased.

But was he really pleased, or was he just being gracious? Was he being rewarded or punished?

Joel hoped Noah would come back to take a full-time job with Fogwire Software.

But he didn't.

Google made him a better offer.

Duh.

Why would Noah accept an offer from Google instead of from Fogwire, which had given him such warm recognition?

Because Google's offer included more *positive, immediate, and certain reinforcers.* But Google's not perfect either. (Read Chapter 20: "Cave People: One Size Does Not Fit All" to learn more.)

The problems with Joel's approach to Noah are many, but here are the most glaring:

1. Joel made the mistake of not giving R+ to Noah, on the questionable grounds that "That's what we're paying him to do." Paychecks get you to show up for work. When people do something well, you'd better give them R+... or maybe your competitor will.

2. Joel made the R+ conditional: "IF you come back to work for us THEN you'll get the stock option." This is a tacit admission that Noah probably had a brighter future elsewhere in view of his million-dollar, home-run idea. Making the reward conditional upon Noah's return, in fact, was punishing to Noah, and it most certainly was

perceived as manipulative by the company. Better to give than receive, Joel. Remember that one; someone very wise said it.

3. Joel chose R+ that was neither positive, immediate, nor certain. The stock options were of *uncertain, unknown value.* How many Silicon Valley start-ups fail? The reward was delayed, and conditional upon Noah's signing up to work full-time for a company that had just proved it punished great performers. (Wonder how Noah felt as he got into his Toyota Corolla to leave work, only to be passed by his boss Joel driving away in the brand-new red Porsche that Noah's idea paid for?)

I agree with you, Noah. Go work for Google. They'll boost your pay 10 percent, no matter how well you perform.

Joel, all you can do for the rest of your life is wonder what might have been.

I hope this section gives you a different perspective on intrinsic or Self-R+. It most certainly highlights a number of flaws in the "pop psychology" of Alfie Kohn and Daniel Pink, who maintain that intrinsic reinforcers are the only answer. My advice is to have someone test that next glass of Pink Kool-Aid before you drink it.

To read the *INC.* story about Joel, scan the QR Code below or visit www.powerofpositivereinforcement.com and click "How Hard Could It Be?"

"What's up with these
young people? Where's
their work ethic?"
—BABY BOOMER MANAGER

FOURTEEN

Who Killed the Work Ethic?

Why don't people pay their dues, the way we did when we first started out?

Post-Depression-era workers were the best. They could be used and abused and would still show up for work the next day, remembering the bread lines and unemployment of their formative childhood years.

That generation has, for the most part, retired.

In their place is a generation of "Latchkey Kids" who remember Mom and Dad being gone a lot.

In the book, *Work with Me,*" authors Debra S. Magnuson and Lora S. Alexander explain the generational differences between the workers of the Great Depression era, the Baby Boomers, and their kids and grandkids known as Gen X and Gen Y.

Boomers brought much of the same work ethic to the job that their Depression-era parents did, but they also enjoyed the prosperity of the post-World War II economy. With both Mom and Dad working, most Gen X and Gen Y kids were raised by Nintendo.

One Gen X says, "I watched both of my Baby Boomer parents drag in tired at 8 p.m. from working all day at their jobs. I'll never do that to my kids."

Ever played Nintendo? I have. It's great fun. You do something, you get R+. You do something else, and you get R+. In short, you get positive feedback and positive reinforcement hundreds of times per minute.

Now, if you were reared as a Latchkey Gen X or Gen Y kid on a steady diet of hundreds of R+ per minute, hour after hour every day, how do you think you'd react to an "old-school, my-way-or-the-highway, sink-or-swim" management style?

You might expect just a little conflict between the four generations of American workers. And that is precisely why the older workers often sigh, roll their eyes, and ask this question about Gen X and Gen Y workers: *"Who killed the work ethic?"*

Managers have ignored great performance for so long that people have become cynical, and the balance of power has shifted toward the worker.

Employee engagement is the passionate goal of many managers now, and rightly so. A study by Towers Perrin (now Towers Watson), a professional services firm specializing in human-resources and financial-services consulting, found employee engagement to be a key driver of every measure of financial success.

The study also showed that the actions of management drive employee engagement, or result in its absence. If superior performance isn't reinforced, people will stop delivering. Maybe that's why fewer than 15 percent of employees today are engaged in their work.

I remember one employee who will always be a hero in my book. When I first started working for my father's company, I was in the shipping department (you name it, I did it, no questions asked).

One day, I decided to extend our concrete drive for our receiving area by pouring the concrete myself. Now, the fact that I had never poured concrete before never fazed me. I had read the "how-to" book, and I was ready to lay concrete.

The concrete truck pulled up. It was July—a horribly hot, high noon in South Carolina. The harder I worked that concrete, the faster it set up. I marvel today at how hard my heart beat as I worked. It's a miracle I didn't pass out.

But it was no use. I had concrete setting up hard, and I couldn't work it out fast enough . . . until that brown UPS truck rolled up with Mac Robinson, the driver for our route. I knew Mac had a lot to do. I knew that UPS gave drivers a quota of stops and that pushed them pretty hard. So when Mac got out of his truck and started helping me work the concrete, I became forever a UPS customer. We laid the concrete that day, with only a few waves and wrinkles that I still smile at as I pass that driveway some 30 years later.

Did Mac face some possible negative consequences for helping me out? I'm sure he did. His boss wasn't on the truck to see my plight. But Mac was an engaged employee, if ever there was one. I will never forget him or his company.

"WILL YOU PAINT THE WALL, PLEASE?"

Leonardo Inghilleri is one of the key people who helped Horst Schulze make the Ritz Carlton a legend in customer service. Leo teaches new employees that the guest experience can either be a plain, white wall, or a masterpiece like the ceiling of the Sistine Chapel. While both surfaces are painted, one is light years beyond the other. Each interaction with a guest at the Ritz Carlton is like a brushstroke in the master painting.

So, Leo tells his staff, no matter what you do, you are helping paint that picture. This connection with the mission helps Leo's new Capella Hotels create that masterpiece experience.

THE DEATH OF A WORK ETHIC

In his book, *How Starbucks Saved My Life*, Michael Gates Gill, a son of privilege, tells how he prided himself on his exalted progression from boarding school through Yale University and into a lofty career with J. Walter Thompson, one of the world's most prestigious advertising agencies.

As he moved through this rarefied environment, he often looked down on people less fortunate, and conveniently labeled them "under-performers."

Then, out of the blue, Gill lost his job, wealth, and family. Then he learned he had a brain tumor. Without health insurance, he desperately sought a job at Starbucks as a last resort.

It became the best job of his life. Here, he began to embrace diversity, and learned to treat others as he would like to be treated.

Gill recalled that at J. Walter Thompson, he had learned that to succeed, he had to cater to his client's every whim.

One of his clients was Ford Motor Company. On Christmas day, while his little children were unwrapping presents, Ford executives insisted that he leave his family immediately for a video shoot. The kids cried and begged him to stay.

He left.

Behold, the Company Man!

Gill gave his all to the agency—until J. Walter Thompson needed a more youthful staff. Then, Gill was fired.

At JWT, the rewards were few, and far between. The expectations were high. Self-motivation and pride carried the day.

But Alfie, I wonder how Gill's children would act if they went to work for JWT?

Would they leave their children crying as he did, simply to meet a client's needs?

Would the intrinsic value of achieving great work make them sacrifice their children and marriages at the helm of success?

I doubt it.

Thank goodness for "work/life balance."

As a final thought, I would like to quote Aubrey Daniels, who said to me one day, "We are all guilty of killing the work ethic, because of our failure as leaders to deliver R+ for desired performance. Who killed the work ethic? We all did."

FIFTEEN
Daughter-of-the-Month

While surveying the employees of one of the top luxury hotel firms in the world, I met Rose, a delightful lady.

Rose was in a focus group I held with some of the hotel employees. I asked her how many times she'd been positively reinforced for something done well during her three years of employment at the hotel.

Her eyes narrowed as she searched her memory.

"Only once, when I was voted 'Best Customer Service Employee-of-the-Year,'" she replied.

"Why?" I asked.

"I don't know," she mused. "They never told me. Maybe it was a survey or something? But the worst part was how they surprised me in front of my peers and told them I was the best, and they weren't. Now two of those ladies won't speak to me."

Rose concluded: "It was the worst day of my life!"

I call this syndrome "Why them? Why not me?"

Rose was singled out for praise at the expense of her coworkers. So they singled her out for punishment. In Australia and New Zealand they describe this as the "Tall Poppy" syndrome, meaning that the tallest poppy in the bunch inevitably gets cut down to size.

For this very reason, and others, Employee-of-the-Month programs are bad news. Any time you pit one employee against all the others, you have a recipe for disaster. Nobody wants to be seen as the "teacher's pet." To make matters worse, publicly recognizing individuals in front of their peers is a surefire way to erode workplace morale and team spirit.

I have two daughters: Daphne and Carli.

What if I pop in one day from a business trip and line them up and say, "Hey Carli, give Daphne a round of applause, 'cause she's Daughter-of-the-Month, and **you're not**."

How's that going to go over?

That's precisely what we do with our employees through Employee-of-the-Month programs and other dumb ideas.

"We decided to let
employees nominate
their peers for R+."
—HR MANAGER

SIXTEEN
Most Likely
to Succeed

Does a "peer-to-peer" employee-driven recognition system really work?

Many leaders think that a peer-nominated "Above & Beyond Star Performer" program delivers all the R+ needed, without the risk of management's being perceived as showing favoritism.

While peer reinforcement is important, it is less than half of the R+ that employees need. The most important kind of R+ can only be delivered by the boss.

So if, as a leader, you say nothing, you are sending a message. And if you say *something* you are sending another message. Since you are pretty much stuck with delivering positive reinforcement or punishment, no matter what you say or do, it is probably wise to be sure you are delivering R+ for the desired behaviors.

While peer-to-peer R+ certainly has value, it's no match for sincere, specific, heartfelt reinforcement from your manager.

So often, peer-to-peer recognition systems are instituted simply to help managers avoid the complex, painful decisions about ways to deliver the right recognition. They can just offload all the headaches of recognition on some employee committee.

While it may be the easy way out (for management), it isn't the best option. When leaders don't understand and embrace the best methods of reinforcement, they set their employee-recognition teams and committees up for inevitable failure, and they fail to harness the human factor fully.

SEVENTEEN
"You Can't Positively Reinforce People If They Hate Your Guts"

Think about it. We can try our best to give specific, focused reinforcement all day long. But if people don't trust us, our reinforcement becomes punishing instead of positive. You can't fake integrity.

FIVE APES AND A BANANA
So I'm sitting at the Sydney Opera House watching the sailboats on the bay as people walk across the top of the bridge. Pretty cool being here in Oz (Aussie-speak for their country). And my dear mate Doug begins to tell me a story about five apes and a banana:

So what you do Bill, is you put four apes in a cage, with a clump of bananas at the opposite end. Apes absolutely love ba-

nanas, more than anything else. Now, the four apes are looking around at each other trying to decide who's the alpha male and who will make the first move on the bananas. Soon enough, the big one decides it's his turn.

And so he begins to saunter up for his tasty prize. At this point you take ice cold water in a fire hose and hose him down and knock him to the back of the cage and continue the hose-down operation on all the apes. And then you have four wet, shivering apes. Now, as much as apes love bananas, they hate being wet.

So now you introduce the fifth ape. You don't want to be that lad, since he walks into the cage with four wet apes on one end and some really juicy bananas on the other. Figuring he's the alpha male, he makes his move on the bananas; and before he takes his second step, the other apes will grab him and drag him to the back of the cage and beat him mercilessly.

Universal Truth: Nobody—not even an ape—wants to get hosed.

THE MORAL OF THE STORY

When you introduce R+ into your culture, you may think you are on a level playing field, but quite often you are not. You're likely to discover that the culture you've stepped into exists somewhere in the R- basement, below the level playing field. Even worse, you may come to work in a toxic culture where years of punishment have created the labor union/management "us/them" mentality. You may be 43 stories below the Ground Floor of R+.

Sometimes, the five-apes-and-a-banana culture is so ingrained that it may seem that even a "bunker buster" of R+ cannot crack it. Understand which floor your culture is on before you start your behavior-change process. An assessment is a good way to start.

Know that some employees will resist your efforts, having been hosed down many times before.

It's important that you never give up as you "turn the battleship" of culture.

Now, most managers think they do a great job of reinforcing their people. To get the real story, you have to ask the employees. And sometimes the real story isn't that pretty.

Many managers need some serious training in how to get R+ right. Rose's boss probably thought that she was doing Rose a big favor by choosing her as Employee-of-the-Year. Sadly, it was Rose's worst nightmare.

Remember how Bob Nelson puts it, "You get the best results by creating a fire within people, not by lighting a fire under them." It's worth repeating.

EIGHTEEN
Teacher's Pet Syndrome

Why do people sometimes resist R+?

Oddly enough, many of the people who resist R+ are the ones who need it the most. When given positive feedback, the "resisters" may respond with any or all of the following:

- "Aw, what I did was nothing."
- "You don't have to tell me that, I'm fine without it."
- "Just put it in my paycheck."

Leo Inghilleri, (one of the founders of Ritz Carlton), now with West Paces Consulting, once told me about an incident at the opening of a new luxury hotel in Europe. The management team began giving positive feedback to employees for their customer-service behaviors. As Leo smiled and told one lady what she'd done right, she gasped, and fainted. The shock at receiving an actual compliment from management was too much for her.

Leo's conclusion after training thousands of employees to deliver service the Ritz Way: "Positive reinforcement and feedback works anywhere you go in the world, *and it works even better outside of America, since most of these workers have worked lifetimes without hearing praise from their bosses.*"

Just after desegregation in the rural Deep South, I went to a really tough Southern school. I learned pretty quickly that you had to make friends fast, and watch your back. I also found that if you stood out as different in any way, it would cause you some serious heartburn.

For example, if the teacher liked something you did, and told the rest of the class how great that was, you were going to get pounded at recess. So getting public reinforcement from my teacher meant I would be punished by my classmates at recess.

It was kind of like I was the fifth ape. I learned quickly that the other kids would punish me if I went for the "bananas." That's how I learned to duck positive reinforcement and recognition. I had become hardwired as an "R+ resister." By age 12, when someone paid me a compliment, I insisted that I really didn't feel that I had done as well as I should have. One day, my dad offered me some advice: "Son, when someone pays you a compliment, accept it."

In that one sentence my dad taught me how to respond to praise and reinforcement. I'm glad he said what he did. I'll never forget it.

How many of us have the "five-ape" and "teacher's pet" syndromes preserved in our memories through childhood experiences such as mine? Plus, we've all known bullies or bosses who used flattery and praise in attempts to manipulate us into doing something we found to be unpleasant.

These are just a few reasons that R+ gets a bum rap sometimes.

Remember what we learned in Chapter 17: You can't positively reinforce someone who hates your guts.

Lack of trust makes R+ harder to give and get. So all the people who misuse and abuse reinforcement have made those honest leaders among us face an uphill battle.

Uphill, yes, but insurmountable, no.

NINETEEN
Pink Cadillacs

He was dead serious. He felt employees should never be rewarded with tangible items of any sort.

But was he right?

Is verbal praise really all it takes? This manager thought so. Like many others, he believed that all we need is an effective way to deliver verbal praise and reinforcement: social reinforcers.

For a time, I thought this might be all we needed too.

True, it's critical that we get the social reinforcers right: the smile, the eye contact, the sincerity, the immediacy after the event. These reinforcers are instant-on, ready when we need them, just in time, and we never have to stock or ship them.

But don't tell me that gifts are obsolete.

THE EMPTY RING BOX

A consultant I know insists that rewarding people with gifts robs them of their intrinsic motivation.

"Just get the social reinforcers right, Bill," he told me. "Forget the gifts."

Was he right? Is it true that gifts and money delivered for specific achievements are wrong? I wondered.

"WILL YOU MARRY ME?"

The eager young suitor drops to his knees and gazes into the young lady's eyes.

"Honey, I love you so much that I know the intrinsic value of this social reinforcement is all you need," he says, as he opens the black-velvet ring box.

Her eyes light up—until the box opens with no ring inside.

"I know that the internal reinforcement of your love for me means more to you than any diamond ring ever could, dear. And that $5,000 I saved will come in real handy on that new Jet Ski I just bought. *Will you marry me, please?*"

How many of you think she'll accept the proposal?

Clearly, the right gift at the right time enhances and accelerates the R+ we want to deliver.

AN ARMY OF PINK CADDIES

Mary Kay Ash, the late entrepreneurial cosmetics CEO, built a devoted army of salespeople who can each win the highest sales honor—a pink Cadillac. Legend has it that she wanted to recognize one of her best performers with a new Cadillac, and while picking it out, she produced a compact containing her pink Mountain Laurel blush. She asked the dealer to paint the car the color of the blush. The pink Cadillac was a hit, and in some years, Mary Kay Ash presented up to 9,000 of them to her employees in recognition of their excellent performance.

Mary Kay used pink Cadillacs the way the military uses medals: as an honor that goes beyond words, as a symbol of achievement.

A study at the University of Waterloo in Canada concluded that tangible reinforcers linked to social reinforcers enhanced the impact of R+ by a factor of four.

Maybe that's why I still remember the ice cream, and mom's warm smile of approval. Heck, I'll bet that consultant who disdains tangible gifts has a diploma on his wall to give him intrinsic motivation.

TWENTY

CAVE People:
One Size Does
Not Fit All

"We do a great job at employee recognition," said the Human Resource manager at a large hospital.

"That's good to know," I said. "How do you go about recognizing great performers?"

"Well, we do a picnic quarterly and select the Employee-of-the-Quarter for each department. Then there's our year-end Christmas party, where we choose an Employee-of-the-Year," she replied.

"How is that working for you?" I asked. "Have you had a positive impact on statistics indicating the satisfaction of your employees and patients? Can you measure and quantify your employee engagement? Did your system really change anybody's behavior?"

She glared back at me in silence. Apparently I had hit a nerve. I had a pretty good idea that this meeting was over.

Oops, I think I did it again. I felt kind of bad for being too direct. It appeared that my honesty had gotten me in trouble yet another time.

But in fact, this company was heavily entrenched in "one-size-fits-all" recognition, which does more harm than good.

By now, if you've read Chapter 15: "Daughter-of-the-Month," you understand clearly why an Employee-of-the-Month, of-the-Quarter, or of-the-Year is a bad idea.

Any time we set up one employee to win at the expense of everyone else, we have given our workplace culture a suicide pill. Competition is what we do in the marketplace, not what we do with our coworkers. Our team rises and falls based on the *team's* achievements.

Most managers have seen the problems inherent in the "Employee-of-the-Month" approach, and so they've swung the recognition pendulum to the opposite extreme: one-size-fits-all. Too bad these managers skip right over the little sweet spot in the middle that I call "behavior-based recognition."

In "one-size-fits-all" cultures, everybody gets exactly the same thing, whether deservedly or not. You get the same barbecue dinner as I do, despite the fact that you may contribute three times the value to the organization that I do.

Google garnered a lot of negative publicity when it granted a "one-size-fits-all" 10 percent pay raise to every worker in the company, regardless of the individual's contributions. But let's not just pick on Google; almost every company in the world has a pay system with a huge Achilles heel. People (for the most part) get paid to show up at work. Their pay is not tied to their performance or to the viability of their company's product in the marketplace.

We need to recognize the distinction between R+ and the one-size-fits-all approach. If you're providing positive feedback, reinforcement, recognition, and rewards that result in an increase in the behavior you want, that's R+. If your program results in a drop in the behavior you want, it's punishment.

So our well-meaning managers have bestowed on their workers a plethora of picnics, barbecues, T-shirt giveaways. and endless other celebrations to commemorate safety, sales, quality, and other milestones. In these systems, usually a lagging indicator (result) is rewarded and, in the case of safety, we sometimes see the bad effects of injury-suppression, hiding, under-reporting and the like.

This Pandora's Box of bad side effects is one reason that the behavioral community often argues against incentive systems.

"Hey, the one-size-fits-all method is at least better than Employee-of-the-Month method," says the manager.

But is it really?

Not in my book.

Here's why:

As I've traveled the world speaking, I've used CAVE People to explain why one size does not fit all.

Everywhere I've been, every manager has employees who are CAVE People. I'll bet you have some too.

What's a CAVE person?

My good friend Kenny Sawyer says they are "**C**itizens **A**gainst **V**irtually **E**verything."

They whine and complain. They sleep through training meetings. They break the safety rules and drag down your team. They insult your clients and bring your customer satisfaction scores down.

Thank goodness, you also have people who are hard workers—those above-and-beyond people who value their jobs and deliver safe, quality products or guest experiences.

So you have three distinct groups in every culture: 1) High Performers, 2) Average Performers, and 3) CAVE People.

Given this cross-section of the average workforce—High Performers, Average Performers, and CAVE people—how have we attempted to motivate and reward them?

We've used one-size-fits-all reward systems, which go kind of like this:

"Er, excuse me folks; we would like to recognize your performance this past quarter.

"Now, I know that you High Performers have done everything we've asked of you, and a whole lot more.

"You CAVE people have slept through every training meeting, broken every safety rule, and missed every deadline we've given you.

"And you average folks, well, what can I say? Thanks for being average."

Now the manager holds a card over his head.

"So, in honor of our team achievements, we're awarding everybody a $100 gift card, and we're going to have a picnic this Saturday, plus a free T-shirt if you show up. Great job people!"

Hold on.

Wait a second.

If you adopted this one-size-fits-all method, did you just positively reinforce your high performers, or did you punish them? (Hint: the answer starts with *P*.)

Let's pretend that you are one of the high performers and I'm a CAVE person working in the cubicle next to you—close enough for each of us to know which role the other fits.

Now suppose that, during "Employee Happiness Day," you happen to be in the steak dinner line, filling up your plate, and

I'm right behind you. You think about all the effort you made to help improve performance, and all the things I didn't do.

Then you notice that my steak is just as big as yours.

How does that make you feel? (punished, right?)

So, when you use one-size-fits-all systems, you *punish* your best workers.

How about the CAVE people? Did you just reinforce their bad behavior?

Yep, you sure did.

You effectively said, "Hey go out and take more shortcuts, break more rules, sleep through more training, and you will be rewarded just as much as our High Performers."

And your Average Performers will actually be encouraged to become CAVE people, thinking, "It does no good to work hard around here. Nobody will notice anyway. Look at those poor High Performer guys. What suckers they are!"

The problem with one-size-fits-all recognition is clear.

Yet, the practice is repeated day in, day out, at millions of companies around the world, in the form of picnics, profit-sharing, gain-sharing, goal-sharing, and the like.

Does it improve performance?

No.

So my advice to anyone doing "Employee-of-the-Month" or "One-Size-Fits-All" is to take a hard look at what you're doing and find a strategy linked to performance improvement, on a fair but unequal basis, to everyone.

This means practicing R+: the reinforcement of the behaviors that drive the results you seek.

To achieve the results you want, you need your team to focus on behavior.

TWENTY-ONE
"Business
Is Behavior."

—Aubrey Daniels

Business leaders today share a common dream: to improve business performance and increase profits. In short, great leaders are always in search of better results.

To change our results, we have to change the behaviors of our people.

In my "Green Beans & Ice Cream" sessions with managers, we talk a lot about what makes a great leader. The usual responses are integrity, honesty, dependability, courage, decisiveness, and the like. Every one of these qualities is important.

But there is one leadership quality that everyone overlooks, and in my book, it is the most important.

The way I discovered it was during a chat with Eric Schwartz, who worked, at the time, in city government in Fresno, California.

"Bill, I was amazed at how my supervisors rejected the idea that employees needed R+," he said. "They told me that all we needed to do was to give people a paycheck. I looked them dead in the eye and told them this: If all it takes is a paycheck to get great safety, quality and productivity, what do we need you supervisors for?"

I couldn't have said it better, Eric.

What Eric alluded to was the number one trait of great leaders: the ability to change the behavior of others.

Think about it: If people were going to give us their absolute best safety, quality, sales, production, and customer service automatically, then most managers would be out of a job.

Your success as a leader depends on one thing more than any other: your ability to change the behavior and improve the performance of your followers.

The true test of every leader is what their employees do "in the moment of choice, when nobody is watching."

Since performance improvement is every leader's greatest challenge and opportunity, the art of R+ behavior change is something every one of us should master.

"MY SUPERVISOR IS THE CEO AROUND HERE."

Unfair as it may be, most of what happens on a day-to-day basis for the average employee is dictated not by the CEO or the board of directors, but by the individual employee's supervisor or manager. When you quit your job, you leave your manager, not your company.

Of course, the CEO and senior leadership are involved in enterprise decisions about downsizing, mergers, and the like, but for the most part, it's the frontline supervisor who sets the tone for the employee's perception of the company. And often that perception isn't very pretty.

Remember the story about the lawyer who quit her job to become a waitress? Her boss was always pointing to her mistakes but never complimenting her extra efforts. It was the boss, not the company that caused her to walk away.

Ken Blanchard coined the term, "Leave Alone/Zap" for this management style. This may help explain why Bob Nelson's research showed that 68 percent of employees had never heard the words "Thank you" from their bosses, even though they consistently rank the need for positive feedback as #1 or #2 in job satisfaction.

We all instinctively know that we feel good when we are given sincere, specific, positive feedback. Why then, are fewer than 30 percent of our leaders using it?

Would your company be happy producing a product that worked properly only 30 percent of the time? Why are we willing to tolerate a management system that manages people properly only 30 percent of the time? The sad truth is that without even knowing it, the majority of leaders today are using Leave Alone/Zap management tactics.

TWENTY-TWO
Stuff That Rolls Downhill

Some anonymous soldier once observed that when bad things happen to a leader, something bad inevitably happens to the soldiers in his command. The principle was immortalized in an expression about stuff that rolls downhill.

For many people, the things that "roll downhill" are expected to be unpleasant, negative, or punishing. This is why mergers and acquisitions are so nerve-racking to most people. Experience has taught people that mergers and acquisitions are usually accompanied by layoffs, terminations, and a whole lot of procedural changes that are inherently punishing; they roll down the hill fast.

But it doesn't have to be that way.

Enlightened leaders know that the most powerful things to send "downhill" are positive consequences and feedback.

If we had a special X-ray machine that would show us how work really gets done in a company, we would see billions of little strings that connect the CEO to the president, to the vice president for ops and other vice presidents. From there, the strings would lead through voluminous reports down to the frontline workers. We would finally see these same strings connecting the "get-it-done" workers to one another.

Both positive reinforcement and punishment are constantly passing up, down, and across this network of "feedback neurons" and they allow the organization to think, produce, and act.

To illustrate, let me tell you about Tom.

TOM'S STORY

Tom worked for a large German manufacturing firm with operations all over the globe. One day his chief financial officer received a phone call from the home office. Corporate had mandated that every plant implement a kaizen program—a continuous improvement system aimed at getting ideas from employees to improve quality and efficiency. Apparently, this CFO had failed to implement, and corporate informed him that if he didn't have a system up and running in two weeks he would be looking for a new job. Some stuff had just rolled down the hill—and landed in his lap. It had a bad smell.

In a flurry of activity, the CFO got in touch with a company and ordered materials to launch his new program with a bang. He told everyone at corporate that he had a program in place, and now the pressure was off.

At least until corporate asked why he had received zero improvement ideas.

We were asked to figure out why the wheels had fallen off the CFO's "kaizen."

Tom was one of the line workers we interviewed. He is the type of rare, out-of-the-box thinker that every company dreams of having. I asked Tom what happened with the CFO's program.

"Bill, it's a joke," he replied. "I turned in 31 suggestions to my supervisor, and only one of those ever got reviewed by accounting. They concluded that it saved $532,000. The 30 other ideas are stuck in my supervisor's drawer gathering dust. He told me not to bother him with any more ideas; he was too busy."

Tom's supervisor was being graded by his manager on production and efficiency. Getting 31 ideas from Tom was punishing to that supervisor; now that "stuff" was even rolling uphill.

We suggested that the CFO's duties as coordinator of the continuous-improvement program be turned over to Tom. Our advice was followed, and we helped him to "flatten" the system and ensure that key behaviors were positively reinforced for both supervisors and employees.

I got a phone call from Tom about six months later: "Bill, you'll never believe what we've achieved: a total of 1,382 suggestions and $4 million in savings in one year alone."

I was pleased, but not surprised. Once the correct consequences are in place, there is no limit to what people can achieve.

Sad to say, Tom got a new manager several years later, and the new boss felt that by spending a million dollars on Six-Sigma black belts, he could quickly improve efficiency and quality. Apparently this management strategy, originally developed in 1986 by Motorola, was the new "flavor-of-the-month" that had rolled down the hill.

To make his point, the new boss killed Tom's program and committed the cardinal sin of bad leadership: He failed to provide the rewards he had promised his workers for their ideas. He chose to roll something else downhill too. In less than a month, the resulting lack of trust destroyed everything Tom had worked for years to build.

As of this writing, those million-dollar, Six-Sigma guys have yet to show the first hard dollar of savings. Maybe the company will make Tom plant manager one day.

So we learn from all of this that frontline supervisors mirror their leaders. If senior leaders punish the supervisors, then supervisors will punish the workers. If senior leaders use a positive approach, their supervisors will as well. It all rolls downhill—even the good stuff—and it starts at the top.

Building trust in your workforce is like filling up a bucket of water one drop at a time. Destroying that trust is as easy as kicking over the bucket.

TWENTY-THREE
"Feel-Good" Recognition

Christy works for a medical-equipment repair company. Its nearly 700 employees are scattered across the United States, usually with three-to-five per location. They service medical equipment when it breaks.

"I've just taken over HR, and I'm reviewing our corporate recognition program," she said. "I thought we had an effective system until I surveyed our employees and found that 60 percent of them feel our recognition process is useless."

She explained that the company had seven core values that it was trying to recognize. These were the usual qualities you see represented on those posters bearing pictures of waterfalls and mountains: integrity, dedication, teamwork, persistence, and the like.

Christy's company used a Web system that enabled it to single out a core value a particular employee had exemplified. For instance, when an employee demonstrated teamwork, a recommendation went out that the individual be rewarded. The communication would explain what the employee had done to exemplify that core value. The manager could approve or deny the recommendation. If it was approved, the employee would get a gift card or some similar tangible award. Approval was neither immediate nor certain.

Christy continued: "Our problem is that we have a couple of managers who use the system (and perhaps abuse it), and the others don't use it at all. Peer-to-peer participation isn't what we'd like it to be."

"Can you share with me a real-life example of an employee who was recognized and what the employee did to receive this praise?" I asked her.

"Well, it's a bit hard to piece together, since most of our nominations are vague and non-specific," Christy replied. "But we did have one employee who was asked to repair a vital piece of medical equipment which had failed while the patient was on the operating table. It required a part that would not arrive until 24 hours later, and the patient didn't have that long. The employee went to Home Depot and found a part that would work long enough to save the patient. He really saved a life that day."

"That's a great story," I told Christy. "How often does the average employee get a chance to perform an act like that and be recognized for it? Once a month? Once a year?"

We both decided that the average employee would have maybe one chance in a lifetime to qualify for R+ under her current system, which was also plagued by a lack of precision and specificity as to the behaviors that were going to be reinforced.

We helped Christy see that the most important behaviors are the little ones that happen every day. These are the areas to reinforce on a daily basis.

"YOU'RE NOT WOWING OUR CUSTOMERS!"

Now back to Jan, the customer-service manager who quit her job because management wanted her to "wow" her customers, but gave no guidelines on what constituted "wowing."

The CEO informed her that he and the board had listened to recordings of calls between customers and her team of 300 customer-service people. The brass were disappointed in the team's performance. It just wasn't "wowing" the customers.

"I asked him and the board to give me a list of what they wanted me to change in our script to 'wow' our customers," she told me. "That was a year ago and I haven't heard or seen anything since."

No wonder she quit her job as soon as she found a better option.

SO WHAT DO YOU WANT ME TO DO, EXACTLY?

Since it's so hard for leaders to pinpoint the behaviors that drive improved performance, they often fall into using vague, catch-all terms to describe desired performance. If leaders cannot define the behaviors they need to reinforce, they can hardly expect their followers to do so.

TWENTY-FOUR

Not Another
Baseball Cap

When it comes time to celebrate a success or recognize improvement, you have to figure out what you're going to do. Will it be T-shirts and barbecue this time? Or donuts and coffee? Everyone on the team has a different opinion of what to do. Some will argue for cash, while others sense that cash sends the wrong message. Still others will propose company-logoed baseball caps or coffee mugs.

Many will propose a gift card, and then they will struggle with the handling of the income-tax burden. Will the employee be forced to pay the tax? Or will the company take the huge budget hit of a "payroll gross-up"?

Typically the gift chosen is the one the person with the most political capital likes the best.

Often, we settle on giving them "something with the company logo on it."

This has created an entire industry of companies that warehouse baseball caps, coffee mugs, jackets, pens and the like, all emblazoned with company logos. Now, there's nothing wrong with logo gifts. I have given out thousands of Green Bean pens and other memorabilia as I have spoken around the world, and I've received great feedback.

But the important question is not how the recognition committee feels about logo gifts it chooses. The million-dollar question is, "How do the employees feel about them?" Do they value and appreciate the gifts, and are they using them frequently so that they positively reinforce the desired behaviors? Or do they wind up putting the items on eBay or tossing them in the trash can?

Is the award presented immediately after the behavior occurs, or do we first place the order for shirts, mugs or hats and then hand them out four to six weeks later when everyone has forgotten the milestone we are celebrating?

Many leaders love the idea of their employees marching around with duffle bags and shirts emblazoned with the team logo. But do these gifts change worker behavior for the better? Do the workers find them to be positive, or punishing?

Figure 2 offers some interesting insight.

Figure 2

Tokens used most by large companies*
but judged least effective motivational technique
*COMPANIES WITH $100 MILLION OR MORE IN REVENUE

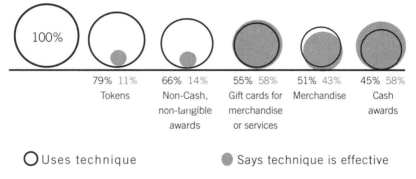

100%					
	79% 11%	66% 14%	55% 58%	51% 43%	45% 58%
	Tokens	Non-Cash, non-tangible awards	Gift cards for merchandise or services	Merchandise	Cash awards

○ Uses technique   ● Says technique is effective

Source: United States Incentive Merchandise and Travel Market Study.
Incentive Federation. Aug 2007

Around the world, I ask my audiences this question: "How many of you have ever received a logoed gift you did not want, need, or use?"

Typically, 98 percent of them raise their hands. And every one of them told the person "Thank you" for their gift, which was quickly trashed. I believe we waste a great amount of time and money giving people "stuff" that they don't need or use.

Can logo gifts be effective? Yes, sometimes. But we need to remember that it is the recipient of the gift who decides whether the gift is positive or punishing.

One company gave out jackets to its workforce, and when it got to the last department, management heard loud complaints from the workers who wanted to know why they were the last to get the jackets.

"You see, they really do like this logo stuff," said the excited plant manager, feeling vindicated in his choice of gifts.

"Well actually, boss," replied his supervisors, "they wanted to put it on e-Bay and sell it, but since the market is already flooded, they are complaining they can't get anyone to bid on them."

Ouch.

In surveys of employees, we routinely see logoed gifts ranked as one of the least effective ways to reinforce behavior.

Figure 3

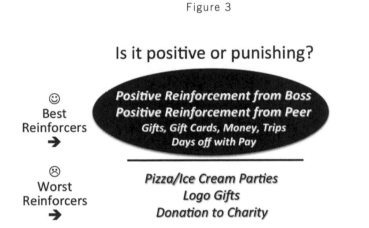

Is it positive or punishing?

☺ Best Reinforcers →

Positive Reinforcement from Boss
Positive Reinforcement from Peer
Gifts, Gift Cards, Money, Trips
Days off with Pay

☹ Worst Reinforcers →

Pizza/Ice Cream Parties
Logo Gifts
Donation to Charity

"Compensation is a right.
Recognition is a gift."
– ROSABETH MOSS-KANTER

TWENTY-FIVE

Isn't a Paycheck Enough?

We hear this quite often from leaders. They spend vast amounts of time and money with consultants to create profit-sharing plans in pursuit of systems that will produce performance improvement. Complex formulas are developed to calculate the payouts, and many employees are clueless about how their system works. While these systems can have impact, they often fail to drive behavior change on a daily basis.

Here are some of the main reasons that these systems fail to produce real behavior change:

- The positive reinforcement usually comes at the end of the year, or (at most) at the end of the quarter, which isn't often enough to change behavior. *Delayed* reinforcers fade into the woodwork the minute an *immediate* reinforcer shows up.

- The rewards are uncertain, and frequently one person's mistake ruins the payout for everyone.

Pay raises tied to annual performance appraisals are delayed reinforcers. They come just once a year—assuming the appraisals are performed in a timely fashion.

Even worse, the raises are highly subjective or uncertain. Since everyone knows that only a select percentage of employees can be given the highest scores, and thus the best pay raises, the system de-motivates and punishes most people.

Bob Nelson has compiled the following figures:

- The typical difference between raises for outstanding employees and those for average employees is 3 percent of base salary.
- Of the workers surveyed, 81 percent said they would receive no reward for productivity increases.
- Of the managers surveyed, 60 percent felt their salaries would not increase should their performances improve.

"Positive reinforcement? Yeah we get that every Friday, Bill."

The chuckles went up from around the meeting room in Anchorage, Alaska, when a supervisor made that comment after the company vice president had introduced me. I was there conducting a workshop on positive reinforcement with about 150 leaders of a large company.

I got a laugh out of it too. Then I asked the audience how many of them agreed that a paycheck was positive reinforcement.

About half of the people said "no" and the others said "yes," or were noncommittal.

"In case you guys haven't noticed it, you don't agree about this," I told them. "And if you can't agree as to whether something as simple as a paycheck is positive reinforcement, how can your team execute on delivering it consistently?"

The laughter was replaced by silence. Nodding heads told me I had made my point.

"Now, I will answer my own question," I continued.

"A paycheck IS positive reinforcement. It reinforces one behavior, and one behavior alone: the behavior of coming to work. If anyone doesn't believe me, I have a little experiment we can conduct. Just give me your paycheck for the next few weeks, and let's see how long you keep showing up for work."

More laughter.

"So, now that we are clear that a paycheck is R+ for coming to work, let me ask you a question. After the paycheck gets me to work, does it also make me perform my work safely? Does it guarantee that I'll give great customer service, quality, or productivity? The answer is no. That is why it takes additional R+ from you leaders to ensure that people perform at their best. My fondest dream is that I will never ever hear another leader say: 'But that's what they are being paid to do.'"

TWENTY-SIX

Is Cash Really King?

Many leaders feel that cash is the most effective motivator, and clearly, cash does influence worker behavior, as long as it is positive, immediate, and certain. In 1943, Abraham Maslow proposed his "Theory of Human Motivation" that centered on a pyramid (Figure 5) representing a "hierarchy of human needs." His theory suggests that once the workers' basic need for income has been met, throwing more money at behavior doesn't always get us better performance.

There are some non-obvious drawbacks to using cash as a motivator. It often becomes expected, and is viewed as part of the compensation package. Thus, when it's removed or replaced, employees are punished and demotivated. Consider these alternate perspectives on the use of money as a motivator:

- University of Waterloo
  In this study, a group of people were asked what type of award would motivate them to finish a task. Some 82 percent chose cash, saying that money would motivate them best. When the study was completed, cash did prove to increase the completion rate on the task, but the people awarded with a non-cash alternative (e.g. a new iPod) improved their performance twice as much as those who earned cash.

- The Neuron Study
  Here, an MRI measures stimulation of the striatum (the brain areas that are linked to pleasure). Interestingly enough, gambling stimulates these areas, as does risk-taking. Money also stimulates these areas. When researchers gave people sincere verbal praise and feedback (R+) they were amazed to see the same part of the brain stimulated.
  Unless your company prints money, you don't have unlimited cash in your budget to use to improve performance. The HR folks may frown at the idea of slot machines in your employee break rooms, and bungee jumping off the corporate office building is probably not going to fly with your legal department.
  You do, however, have an unlimited supply of sincere and positive feedback, and it costs you nothing to deliver it. Mastering the use of this powerful tool will unlock the potential of your team.

- United Parcel Service and the $5,000 Watch
  A UPS manager told me this story: "When our workers

have been five years with the company, injury free, we celebrate by giving them a watch. It's not really fancy. It's just a $250 watch with our safety logo. But many of our people covet this award. In fact, when we promote our young leaders to managers, most of them ask us to wait until they've "gotten their watch" before they'll accept the promotion along with the $5,000 pay raise they would get."

Imagine that: people give up $5,000 in money so they can receive R+ and praise for a job well done!

- IBM and the Six-Figure Suggestion Award Winners
  IBM surveyed its top 23 employees, who were paid more than $100,000 for each innovation that helped the firm compete and improve efficiency. A year later, not one of these employees had submitted another suggestion for improvement. Tom Dupre, who at that time oversaw the IBM suggestion process, concluded that maybe cash wasn't all it was cracked up to be.

- The Payroll Gross-Up "Death Spiral"
  Most companies begin a recognition process with gift cards or other cash substitutes. Unsuspecting managers plan their budgets as usual, blissfully unaware that gift cards come with hidden strings: income taxes. The shock therapy is administered quickly by the tax department, which informs the manager that the $100,000 gift card budget will either result in $50,000 of unexpected income taxes for the employees ("Ouch! You call this a bonus?") or a "payroll gross-up," which means the $100,000 in gift cards will cost the firm $192,000. Math

was never my strong suit, so I usually bring a CPA with me to back up numbers like these. Strange as it may seem, most firms go with the latter, a vastly more expensive option—perhaps to keep the peace.

- Unredeemed Gift Cards

  A Kiplinger Newsletter study reports that more than 40 percent of all gift cards are never redeemed. Add to that the expiration fees and account charges, and you'll see why big banks and retailers love to sell gift cards. When only half of them are redeemed in your store, the other half winds up on your bottom line. This has gone on for years, and of late, Congress is working to fix it. But it has been a windfall for the big retailers and gift card suppliers.

- Poor Oprah

  I'm a big Oprah fan, and so when she surprised 236 people in her audience with brand new cars I was thrilled. What Oprah's team didn't count on were the IRS bills given to every car recipient. When all was said and done, most of them had to sell their cars (punishing) to pay their taxes. Who knew? Many a manager has been caught in the "big ticket item" tax trap.

TWENTY-SEVEN
I Hate
My Boss!

When we talk about positive reinforcement, most people instantly assume that we are talking about managers saying "Good job" and "Thank you." Nothing could be further from the truth.

While these approaches can be positively reinforcing, they can also be punishing. In Saudi Arabia, a young man in one of my classes related that he worked on a project, but knew he had not put the effort into it that he could have. After he delivered his report, his boss told him, "Good job."

The young man said that he was now even more demotivated. He knew his work was substandard, and to have his boss tell him it was "good" made it clear that his boss was either uninterested in his performance, gullible, or simply patronizing him until he could be replaced.

The boss's "Good job" was probably well intended; however the worker found it to be punishing.

A young woman once told me how she felt about "Good job" and "Attagirl!"

"I hate my boss," she lamented. "Every morning I get a text from him that says, 'You're the best' or 'Keep up the good work!'"

"Sounds like a pretty good boss to me," I offered.

"Yes, but I checked with the other girls on my sales team. They get the same text at the exact same time I do."

What could have been R+ had turned to punishment. You can't fake sincerity. And without sincerity, you can't deliver R+.

Positive reinforcement occurs in many forms. But only the recipient can tell us whether what we say or do is really positive or punishing.

TWENTY-EIGHT

Is It Positive
or Punishing?

Well-delivered R+ is positive, specific, and personal. It's not just saying, "Good job."

For instance, several years ago, if you worked at Google, you were allowed free time to pursue any project you wanted to. What a great idea.

Then some Google employees took their "free time" projects, launched new companies, and left Google. This was a punishing event for Google leadership. If I had been Google's CFO, I'd have been tempted to pull the plug on the "free time" policy pretty fast.

The other, more recent, development was that Google became concerned about a "brain drain," wherein its best and brightest were leaving for smaller firms. The media speculated that the thrill and excitement of being part of a start-up had more allure than being with giant Google. To stem this exit, Google announced an across-the-board 10 percent pay increase.

Unfortunately, using a "one-size-fits-all" approach to R+ is dangerous:

- You set a precedent and people come to feel entitled to future 10 percent pay raises.
- Your hardworking people are punished when they see less-productive people getting the same reward they received, without having put forth the extra effort.
- Without meaning to, you are actually sending the signal that what gets rewarded is "sticking it out." Even worse, you are rewarding the low performers by telling them their sub-par performances are just fine.

THE GOLDEN BANANA AWARD

At Hewlett Packard, a manager was thrilled with the work done by an employee. All he had was a banana in his lunch bag. He quickly handed the banana to his employee and the "Golden Banana Award" was born.

Was the banana motivating? Nope.

Did the manager's sincere feedback and appreciation make a positive impact? Yes.

The banana became a symbol of that sincere appreciation. We humans need symbols, place-markers, to help us measure our progress through life.

Many senior leaders have found that just walking out and talking to employees about what is going right and what could be better is a great reinforcer. Quint Studer, the legendary hospital executive, found that by simply asking his nurses how they could improve care, and by relentlessly fixing those things, he could move patient satisfaction from "worst in class" to "best in class."

I did a survey of HR and safety managers to find out what people thought might be positively reinforcing to their employees. Figure 4 shows that the responses were all over the map.

Figure 4

	1 (Least Effective)	2	3	4	5	6 (Most Effective)
Ice cream party or pizza party	22.0% (28)	27.6% (35)	25.2% (32)	19.7% (25)	2.4% (3)	3.1% (4)
Logo'd trinkets such as keychains, t-shirts, ballcaps	23.0% (29)	31.7% (40)	29.4% (37)	9.5% (12)	5.6% (7)	0.8% (1)
Cash	7.8% (10)	10.9% (14)	13.3% (17)	14.1% (18)	21.9% (28)	32.0% (41)
Getting a paid day off from work	4.8% (6)	6.4% (8)	13.6% (17)	17.6% (22)	32.0% (40)	25.6% (32)
Gift cards such as Visa, American Express, Walmart etc	7.8% (10)	10.2% (13)	16.4% (21)	27.3% (35)	22.7% (29)	15.6% (20)
A choice of up to 100,000 items (such as on amazon.com, e.g. iPods, tools, cookware etc.)	11.9% (15)	12.7% (16)	25.4% (32)	19.0% (24)	22.2% (28)	8.7% (11)
Making a donation in your name to a worthy charity.	32.0% (40)	28.8% (36)	24.8% (31)	12.0% (15)	1.6% (2)	0.8% (1)
Positive verbal comments of praise from a coworker about something good that you did.	2.3% (3)	11.5% (15)	15.4% (20)	25.4% (33)	24.6% (32)	20.8% (27)
Positive verbal comments of praise from your supervisor about something good that you did.	2.3% (3)	9.2% (12)	9.9% (13)	17.6% (23)	32.1% (42)	29.0% (38)

"So often we assume that we know what motivates people. In reality all we really know is what motivates ourselves."
— Ken Blanchard

Without a doubt, what motivates you may not motivate me. As mentioned before, but worth repeating, it's up to the recipient to decide whether it's positive or punishing.

TWENTY-NINE
Don't Drink the Pink Kool-Aid

Do rewards and R+ rob us of our internal motivation?

In his book *Drive*, Daniel Pink argues eloquently against external praise and reinforcers, and touts instead the internal drive that makes us excel. He states that incentive programs work when there is a simple, linear formula for the reward.

For example: Do X, and get Y.

Pink maintains that simple tasks can be rewarded and that performance improves rapidly when they are.

The problem, according to Pink, is that more complex tasks, when rewarded, simply do not improve. Pink suggests that we eliminate all rewards for more complex tasks.

Self-motivation is an incredibly powerful force. However, if we carry the Pink logic to its inevitable conclusion, here are some things we would have to do:

- Abolish all grades, awards, and titles such as Judge, Ph.D., Attorney, and Doctor.
- Pay CEOs, presidents, and other top leaders no more than entry-level workers.
- Totally eliminate the Academy Awards, Pulitzer Prizes, Nobel Prizes and other such awards.
- Discontinue bonuses based on sales results, and reduce pay immediately to flat salaries, with no extrinsic rewards based on performance. (Sales is a profession that requires highly complex sets of behaviors.)
- Pay doctors flat annual salaries regardless of their specialties. Brain surgeons should earn no more than general practitioners.

From these few examples, I think it is clear that external reinforcers are here to stay.

There is a ton of data to support the proper use of rewards and external R+.

Lincoln Electric, for example, has used piece-rate pay systems for years, and has found significant gains in productivity using them. But small, unexpected, more frequent reinforcers are the best. A new study by researchers at the California Institute of Technology (Caltech) suggests that when there are high financial incentives to succeed, people can become so afraid of losing their potentially lucrative reward that their performance suffers.

In a study of several test subjects using MRI machines, the researchers determined that small, immediate, frequent rewards drove improved performance in every case, while larger, more variable rewards caused a reduction of performance. Apparently, people become so worried about losing the award that their cognitive ability is diverted to worrying rather than solving the task at hand. I've spent my life helping clients develop systems that deliver the right reinforcers to accelerate behavior change.

Why? Because, bottom line: It works! For decades, such systems have driven superior performance.

Roland Fryer, a professor at Harvard, attempted to improve student performance by paying for grades.

Dr. Fryer's experiment rewarded students in some groups for results (better grades), and in other groups for behaviors (doing homework, getting other students to study with them). Only one practice worked: rewarding behaviors. Rewarding only results produced little or no improvement.

This is not surprising. Behaviorists have known for a long time that positively reinforcing leading indicator behaviors— behaviors that influence results down the line—is much more effective than focusing solely on the results of past behavior.

To read the Roland Fryer study,
scan the QR Code below or visit
www.powerofpositivereinforcement.com

KIDS & PIZZA

Most people in the "anti-rewards" community cite research based on rewarding school children with pizza when they read a desired number of books.

They admit that kids do read more books when rewarded, but they quickly point to a loss of interest in reading after the rewards are removed.

I believe there is a very simple explanation for this, and I learned about it from my good friend, Bob Veazie. Bob and I were talking about "equity" in a relationship, and how we all constantly assess every relationship, comparing what we put into it with what we get out of it. We do this with our parents, our children, our spouses, our friends, and yes, with our employers.

When we feel that the equity is in balance, we are happy to perform. But when we feel that we are not getting a fair deal, we are unhappy with the relationship. This inequity, if not corrected, ends in divorce, loss of friendship, or in finding a new job with a new employer, whom we hope will give us that fair deal.

Is it possible that the kids in the pizza study were punished when their "employer" took away a promised reward?

Is it possible that they, in turn, "punished" their employer (the researchers at the school) by reducing their performance?

When my daughter Carli was in the second grade, she enrolled in an incentive program called "Book it." Basically, she had to read about 100 boring books that she couldn't choose herself (punishment) to get a coupon for a free pizza.

She smiled proudly when she brought me the coupon. I still have it in my desk drawer somewhere. I guess I'm a slacker parent.

When we look through Carli's eyes at the way it all went down, here's what becomes apparent:

- Carli had to read a lot of boring books that she didn't get to choose (lack of autonomy).

- Carli brought me the piece of paper for free pizza, and I smiled and congratulated her.
- I forgot the paper, so Carli never got the reward she was promised (punishing).

Let's compare Carli's pizza experience with her enjoyment of a video game I bought her.

I watched her in our den and marveled at her skill. She stayed on it nonstop for a week and whipped it. (My reflexes won't ever match hers.)

I saw how the game provided her with hundreds of positive reinforcers. No pizza required. It was amazing.

By the way, Carli wasn't robbed of any intrinsic motivation. She had beaten that game, and I expect when another one catches her fancy, she'll whip that one.

The problem with the pizza/book example isn't that incentives don't work. Rewards do improve performance, and the study concluded that even a lame incentive like "maybe-you'll-get-pizza-if-your-dad-doesn't-forget" will improve performance.

But when the children in the study were "paid" to read books (no matter how lame the pizza prize was), then the relationship automatically became "employer/employee." The assigned work would lead to pay in the form of points that would be redeemable for a "pizza paycheck." The "paycheck" increased the kids' book-reading behavior; thus it was positive reinforcement for that behavior. When the paycheck was removed, the equity was altered, and there was now inequity.

The kids were thinking, "What's in it for me? If you used to pay me for reading books and you no longer do, then you are being unfair. Therefore I will only read books that I truly want to read."

In the workplace, we have no choice but to understand and obey the laws of equity and inequity. They take effect the minute we hand people their first paychecks.

We can enhance performance greatly by using R+ to increase the behaviors that lead to success.

By the way, other researchers have reviewed the same data that Daniel Pink and Alfie Kohn used, and they have come up with a totally different conclusion about the data.

Judy Cameron's study, "The Myth Continues," examined reams of data and concluded that unexpected rewards or "gifts" in fact do not rob people of internal motivation, but they do increase performance.

Giving a person an "unexpected reward" that is specifically linked to a certain behavior reinforces the behavior, increases it, and results in no loss of self-motivation.

It's when we give people something they didn't earn that we see "entitlement" occur.

So surprise people and tell them they did it right!

Make sure your reinforcement systems require people to do something. Avoid systems that reward people for what would happen anyway.

IN SUMMARY:

If we don't accept the value of extrinsic R+, we should eliminate all CEO bonuses, pay raises, Academy Awards, grades, scorekeeping at athletic events, and much more.

Of all the consultants who preach against external R+, how many are willing to give up their speaking fees and honorariums?

THIRTY

Chocolate, Vanilla, or Strawberry? The Great Debate

The most powerful source of motivation is a subject of endless debate. Whether it's Oprah Winfrey, Daniel Pink, or Alfie Kohn, the controversy about what motivates human performance rages on.

Many will argue that rewarding good performance is wrong. They suggest that even a soccer mom jumping up and down and screaming with glee when her five-year-old scores a point is robbing that child of the motivation to play the game.

Hmmm . . .

To clear up the muddy water, I offer you the following simple model:

All kinds of R+ fall into three categories. I like to think of them as ice cream cones—vanilla, strawberry, and chocolate. (By now, you've probably figured out that I like ice cream.)

The three flavors of R+ are...

- *Tangible*
- *Social*
- *Self*

Each of these has its relative strengths and weaknesses, and they all play powerful roles in human motivation. Understanding and embracing all of them is the path to performance improvement.

TANGIBLE R+

When you applied for your current job, what was the first question you asked your potential employer? You probably asked what the paycheck was going to be. After that, you asked about benefits, vacation days, sick days, and the like. Tangible reinforcers form a critical first-level "foundation" that needs to be in place if the other kinds of R+ are to be developed. There are many forms of tangible R+, and each of these appeal to people in varying degrees. Some examples are cash awards, paychecks, stock options, trips, gifts, logo gifts, gift cards, and time off from work with pay. While many would say that cash is king of all tangible R+, the research proves otherwise. As we pointed out earlier, a paycheck is R+ for one behavior primarily: showing up for work. Once you are at work, the paycheck has done its job. It takes other kinds of R+ to get the performance lift we desire.

The Catch:

All too often, companies set up payment systems that are "one-size-fits-all." These systems reward people with more pay regardless of whether they produce any real value to the organization. Google's across-the-board 10 percent pay raise is a glaring and expensive example of this approach. It will undoubtedly foster "entitlement mentality" and an expectation of easy-to-get bonuses in the future.

SOCIAL R+

Once a person is coming to work consistently to earn a paycheck, we can add additional reinforcers to boost performance. These can be in the form of additional tangible R+ such as gifts, gift cards, and bonus pay. We can also introduce the idea of social reinforcers.

There are many kinds of social reinforcers. Some of them are positive. And some of them are punishing.

Employee-of-the-Month programs are punishing for most people. Here are some ways you can provide social reinforcers that are positive or rewarding:

- Ask individual employees for input and listen actively to their responses.
- Empower someone to fix a problem.
- Give specific, positive, verbal feedback on what a person did correctly.
- Allow freedom to work from home (assuming home is a happy place).

And there are more.

Bob Nelson wrote a whole book on low-cost forms of social R+. Delivering social R+ is both an art and a science. Done well, it can touch someone's heart. Done poorly, it will burn the relationship forever (see Chapter 27, "I Hate My Boss.")

The Catch:

The Achilles heel of social R+ is this: you can't positively reinforce someone who hates your guts. I remember one supervisor who was like Terry Tate, the villain of the Reebok Super Bowl commercial (see Chapter 4: Does Punishment Really Work?). The supervisor was a true punisher of his people. Faced with a unionization attempt, the management team suddenly "got R+ religion" and decided to have an Employee Appreciation Day, with steak dinners for all employees and their families. Even though the "Terry Tate" supervisor was despised by his people, he was placed in charge of grilling the steaks. As the individual workers came up to him with their plates already heavily laden, he put a steak on each plate. One by one, the employees dumped their plates on the supervisor's shoes. They knew he wasn't sincere, and they resented his attempts at manipulating their behavior. The union campaign was successful. The "five-apes-and-a-banana" mentality caused that management team a lot of pain and expense. As Bob Coleman, CEO of Riegel Textiles once said, "People who get unions deserve them."

SELF R+

Self-reinforcement is a powerful force. Beholding it at work is awe-inspiring. Operating under self-R+, we humans are at our best. We are the firefighter running into the Twin Towers on 9/11, or perhaps the soldier who jumps on top of the grenade to save his comrades. In such cases of courage and heroism, human beings facing almost certain, immediate, and negative consequences are driven by a much stronger self-reinforcer—the internal reinforcement of sacrifice for another. Self-reinforcement develops over time, as people consistently receive adequate amounts of both tangible and social R+.

The Catch:

As we pointed out earlier in the story about Leo Inghilleri (Chapter 14: Who Killed the Work Ethic?), some people are very highly self-motivated around work. Others are far more passionate about hunting, fishing, motorcycle riding, knitting, painting, gardening—you name it. We haven't yet invented a way to measure reliably who is and who isn't self-reinforced today at work. *Self-reinforcement*, by its very definition, is something that you can do only for yourself. Many of the great self-help speakers, such as Anthony Robbins and Brian Tracy, focus on this area.

MASLOW'S HIERARCHY

Maslow's hierarchy of needs, illustrated in Figure 5, actually points to the existence and role of the three flavors of R+. His theory says that the first things people need are the basics: food, money, shelter, clothing—all are forms of tangible R+.

Once these needs are met, we are then looking for social reinforcers, such as positive reinforcement from peers, managers, families, and friends—social R+.

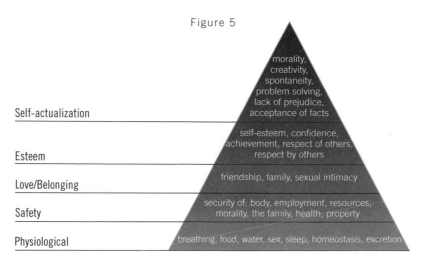

Figure 5

Self-actualization

morality, creativity, spontaneity, problem solving, lack of prejudice, acceptance of facts

Esteem

self-esteem, confidence, achievement, respect of others, respect by others

Love/Belonging

friendship, family, sexual intimacy

Safety

security of: body, employment, resources, morality, the family, health, property

Physiological

breathing, food, water, sex, sleep, homeostasis, excretion

Once all of these needs are met, we are looking to "self-actu-alize"—to engage in things that allow us to reinforce ourselves positively. A wise man once said that it is better to give than to receive. Whether it's the billionaire donating his fortune to help fight cancer, or a volunteer in the hospital who helps a family deal with grief, what you are seeing is people engaging in behavior that produces some level of internal or self-reinforce-ment—self-R+.

The Reinforcement Continuum model (Figure 6) helps us to see how we respond to the three kinds of R+.

Figure 6

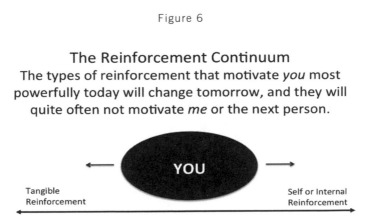

The Reinforcement Continuum
The types of reinforcement that motivate *you* most powerfully today will change tomorrow, and they will quite often not motivate *me* or the next person.

When we first go to work at a new job, we are primarily en-gaging in that behavior to get a paycheck; so tangible R+ is the most important. Over time, as we get to know our coworkers and managers, and as we develop relationships and trust, they will be able to influence our behavior positively using social re-inforcers. Eventually, we develop self-reinforcers for ourselves to continue in the desired habits.

Getting an employee to this level is a slow process, and quite often someone steps in to derail it. Suppose a worker is behaving and performing at the highest level. Then the company announces downsizing, pay cuts, and more work to be done by fewer people.

Yep, the process just got derailed. The worker will slide down the scale of cynicism, performing just well enough to get a paycheck. As soon as another job offer opens up, the employee is lost, gone to another employer.

ALL OF THE ABOVE

So which kind of R+ is best? All of them are. It depends on the performer. Can we get behavior change by using only social R+? Sure we can. You can get to Alaska from Florida on a bicycle if you are determined enough and patient enough. But you can get there a lot faster if you hop on a plane.

I'm not in business to get performance improvement and behavior change slowly. I'm interested in getting it faster than my competitors, and sustaining it better than they can. If you feel the same way, be sure you embrace all three flavors of R+ in your leadership systems.

THIRTY-ONE

Empowering
Employees Is R+

Command & Control is Punishing

During the 1960s and 1970s, American textile companies were being squeezed in the death grip of cheaper offshore labor. One by one, in small towns all over the Southeast, the factories were shuttered and closed. Places such as Sylacauga, Alabama and Lancaster, South Carolina became ghost towns, as production was moved to South and Central America. This decline was the beginning of a larger erosion of American manufacturing capacity, with a huge loss of jobs and a negative impact on the U.S. economy.

While the war against cheap overseas labor was eventually lost, some incredible battles were won along the way.

One winner was Riegel Textile's CEO, Bob Coleman, who made the statement quoted in the preceding chapter: "People who get unions deserve them." Unlike many of his "command-and-control" old-school peers, Bob learned to tap the innovation and creativity of his people, achieving amazing results. He was an early pioneer of the Zero Defects concept, wherein a team of employees, called an "advisory board," identified opportunities to improve quality, efficiency, and safety. These Zero Defects teams were the forerunners of quality circles and the "lean manufacturing" movements of today.

Bob subscribed to the theory that nobody knows the job better than the person who does it eight hours a day.

Using his Zero Defects secret weapon, Bob was able to purchase a textile mill and take it from 72 percent efficiency to 96 percent.

Why does empowering people to change their surroundings have such huge impact? Research shows that one of the key drivers of employee satisfaction (read R+) is "being able to make a difference at work." Giving people the autonomy to change the process to remove negative and punishing consequences, is a huge, untapped source of positive reinforcement.

In his book, *It's Your Ship*, Michael D. Abrashoff discovered the same lessons learned by Coleman. Rising out of the Navy's bureaucracy, he was finally given command of the destroyer *Benfold* in the Pacific Fleet. During the change-of-command celebration in which Abrashoff took over, the new skipper detected contempt for the old commander in the ranks of the 310-man crew. He made up his mind to be a different kind of leader and prove to his subordinates that this was not their fathers' Navy. He had noted that fewer than 30 percent of the enlisted men signed up for new hitches after ending their tours of duty. This turnover was a huge waste of taxpayer funds.

Early on, he scheduled interviews with five crew members every day, taking notes:

"Why did you join the Navy?"

"Are you married?"

"Tell me about your kids."

"What are we doing here that we could do better?"

"Why do we do things the way we do them?"

"Is there a better way?"

Not only did he spend a lot of time asking people for their ideas; he also communicated his own thoughts to his crew, using the ship's PA system. Silence breeds mistrust of leadership he reasoned. In fact, he communicated so much and so well that his crew nicknamed him "Mega Mike."

Periodically, to break up the monotony of shipboard life, the crew organized a grill-out party at the stern of the ship. Under the old commander, enlisted men had been required to go through the food line only after the officers had filled their plates and retired to their special mess hall.

One day without saying a word, Commander Abrashoff went to the back of the line, while the rest of his officers were at the front. They motioned for him to come up front, but he declined. If the food ran out, he said, he would go without. Next, he began eating with the enlisted men, instead of with the officers, asking questions and learning all the time.

Before long, guess what? The other officers began following his example, bringing about a huge culture change and eliminating the class society that had been established.

Did listening to people pay off?

You bet it did.

Under Michael's command, the *Benfold* went from 30 percent staff retention to 100 percent. It became the "go-to" ship in the Navy, with unprecedented accuracy and reliability. The crew was allowed to implement radical new ideas that greatly improved efficiency and reliability.

The lesson is clear.
The truly powerful leaders are those with the confidence
to delegate power to those who are beneath them.
They are confident their people will follow them
whether they are standing there or not.

THIRTY-TWO

What Makes
a Great Leader?

Take a minute before turning this page, and write down 10 core traits of great leaders. (No peeking on the next page)

1. _____
2. _____
3. _____
4. _____
5. _____
6. _____
7. _____
8. _____
9. _____
10. _____

In the leadership courses I teach, here are the traits most commonly listed:

1. Good communication skills
2. Trustworthiness
3. Willingness to listen
4. Knowledge and experience
5. Good attitude
6. Accountability
7. Ability to motivate
8. Integrity
9. Courage
10. Ability to stay organized
11. Ability to inspire respect

How do they match your list?

My point is this: Almost everyone agrees on what good leaders must do, and how they must act.

In fact, here is what some of the greatest leaders have said:

"There are two things people want more than money: recognition and praise."
—Mary Kay Ash

"Trust, not technology, is the issue of the decade."
—Tom Peters

"Nobody cares how much you know until they know how much you care."
— John Wooden,
UCLA basketball coach

But there is one quality of leaders that trumps all the others, and it is the one that nobody guesses.

To help you identify it, fill in the blanks here:

- If every employee gave us perfect human performance, we wouldn't need _____
- The Measure of a Leader is what the followers do in the moment of _____ when nobody is _____
- The most important ability of leaders is the_____ _____ the _____ of their followers.

See the answers on the next page.

To help you identify the leadership quality that trumps all others, see the completed sentences (from the previous page) below:

- If every employee gave us perfect human performance, we wouldn't need managers.
- The Measure of a Leader is what the followers do in the moment of choice when nobody is watching.
- The most important ability of leaders is the ability to change the behavior of their followers.

So as a leader, only one thing really matters: What your people do when you leave. This quality may be defined as "leadership that sticks."

That and that alone defines your ability to deliver and sustain R+ to drive high performance.

As the graphic below illustrates, employee engagement drives the engine of business success. And R+ drives employee engagement. In short, R+ is the fuel you put in the tank of your corporate culture.

Figure 7

Positive Reinforcement is the missing link!

But instead of providing the reinforcers that drive great performance, most managers use Leave Alone/Zap. What is that?

Remember the highly paid lawyer who quit her job to become a waitress?

Her reason was as follows:

"My boss says *something* 100 percent of the time when I make a mistake. And when I put forth extra effort, he says *nothing* 99 percent of the time."

Apparently, she just wanted to work in a culture of people who actively cared about her and reinforced her positively.

Wayne, who works for one of the largest retailers in the United States, tells this story:

I helped a woman the other day in the Garden section. Later, I found out that she was so impressed with my help and service that she went to my manager and told him that she would only be coming to our store from now on, even though it wasn't the one closest to her house. I never got any recognition for that, not even a "Good job." It's not like I expected a raise; just a "Thank you." What kind of incentive do I have to go "Above and Beyond" if I can't even be appreciated or acknowledged when I do?"

Figure 8 depicts the various "buckets" that your employees fit into. Let's hope your training systems are effective, so that people are clear on their mission and are equipped with the tools and skills they need to do the job. Assuming you have done your homework here, then none of your people fall into the first bucket: "I can't do it." That leaves three buckets remaining: Non-compliant, Compliant, and Committed.

Figure 8

Phases of Behavior Change

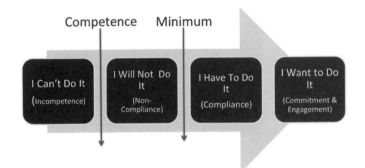

Where do you want your culture?

The answer is obvious: You want commitment. You want people who deliver safety, quality, production, and client satisfaction "in the moment of choice, when no one is watching."

But, how do you move people from non-compliance to commitment?

The sad truth is that most of our managers use the tool we all learned from the police: Leave Alone/Zap.

Leave Alone/Zap does produce a behavior change—at least temporarily. You can see it while you're riding down the Interstate. If you're like me, you and everyone else are driving 10 miles per hour over the speed limit. Guess what? That makes you *non-compliant,* as Figure 9 shows.

Figure 9

Phases of Behavior Change

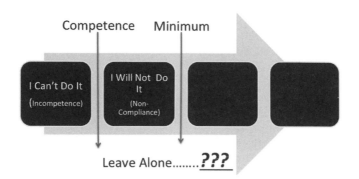

This continues until you see a police officer pointing a radar gun at you. To avoid the "Zap!" what do you do?

You hit the brakes. And so now, to avoid the Zap! you are Compliant (Figure 10).

Figure 10

Phases of Behavior Change

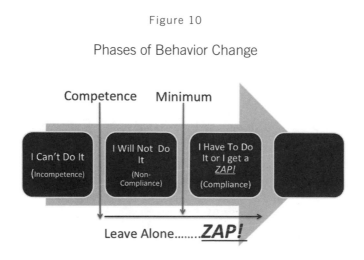

This newfound "religion" you have adopted is short-lived however. About 60 seconds after you pass the cop you breathe a sigh of relief—"Whew! He didn't get me"—and then what do you do?

You hit the gas. Once again, you are *non-compliant.*

The same scenario plays out billions of time a day:

- The students in a noisy classroom misbehave until the teacher enters the room.
- A group of employees slacks off and chit chats until someone tips them off that the boss is coming.

The point is that Leave Alone/Zap fails to produce behavior change in the "moment of choice, when nobody is watching." It doesn't get you commitment; nor does it get you employee engagement.

THE POWER OF R+

But positive reinforcement does lead to that commitment, and a whole lot more.

Figure 11

Phases of Behavior Change

So how well does your management system do at delivering the positive reinforcement people need and crave?

By now you may be getting the picture that your management system has more than its fair share of Leave Alone/Zap.

You are probably thinking that you'd like more positive reinforcement in your culture . . . and a whole lot less Leave Alone/Zap!

But how do you get from where you are to where you want to be?

That is the million-dollar question.

And I'm going to answer that for you.

But first, I'd like to ask you to look in the mirror.

Figure 12 defines the R+ Spectrum, the quest for R+.

Figure 12

Where is your culture?

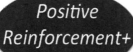

Company A: Magic
Inconsistent reinforcement,
Leave alone/ZAP! Some
managers do it. Most do not.

Company B: Strategic
Consistent measurement
and delivery of positive
reinforcement for the
behaviors that drive
world class results.

In your journey, where is your culture? You have only two choices: Company A or Company B. Which company sounds like yours?

COMPANY A:

"To be honest, when it comes to positive reinforcement, we pretty much rely on MAGIC. When we get it right, it's kind of like pulling the R+ rabbit out of the hat. We're amazed at the results. But it's pretty much a hit-and-miss thing around here. We have an inconsistent definition of what positive reinforcement is; we have our fair share of "Leave Alone/Zap" managers, and we have no real way to measure how well we are doing at delivering R+ to our team."

Or,

COMPANY B:

"I'd say that we are STRATEGIC with R+. We have a clear and consistent definition of what positive reinforcement is, and we execute daily on a strategy of delivering it—from the CEO to the mail room. Here's the report to prove it."

It really doesn't matter where you are on the PR+ Spectrum. The only thing that matters is where you want to be. And that is as far toward the Company B model as you can go.

Watch the "All Over It" video at the QR Code below or visit
www.powerofpositivereinforcement.com

THIRTY-THREE

Why Green Beans & Ice Cream?

The lesson Mom taught me about green beans and ice cream ranks with the most important lessons I've learned in life.

Mom figured out what she needed from me, and in her own very special way she got me to want to do it.

You can put Mom's system to work in your team.

First, you have to *pinpoint* the behaviors you want, and positively reinforce them *immediately* when you see them.

Decide what you want people to do. Focus on the behaviors that drive the results you need. Training has a place, but positive reinforcement is the most powerful factor in sustaining high performance. Speed-limit signs, by themselves do not stop speeders. But consequences do. Positive consequences are always better than punishing ones.The trick is to leverage positive consequences to get people where you want them and to put an end to the negative consequences that shut down and stifle your team, preventing it from performing at its best.

As clear as the model in Figure 13 is, few leaders embrace it. Just ask their employees. The vast majority of today's workers (more than 70 percent) will tell you that they have never heard a "Thank you" from their leadership team (supervisors, managers, executives).

Figure 13

The PR+ Behavior Change Model

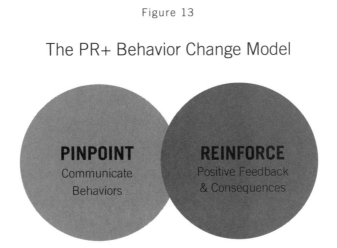

PINPOINT
Communicate
Behaviors

REINFORCE
Positive Feedback
& Consequences

Pinpoint + Reinforce = Behavior Change ™

Find specific things to reinforce positively every day in the actions of people with whom you live and work. Make sure your positives far outweigh the negatives. Remember you need four positive comments for every one negative comment—just to stay even. This doesn't imply that you have to find something negative to say, but that if you do have to correct or even punish, at least four positive comments are necessary to maintain positive performance change.

The book *Chicken Soup for the Soul* by Jack Canfield and Mark Victor Hansen contains a touching story about positive reinforcement that saved the life of a suicidal teenager.

I would like to share that story with you
with the QR Code below or visit
www.powerofpositivereinforcement.com

Yes, that day with Mom and Green Beans & Ice Cream changed my life forever. I know that as you focus on giving positive reinforcement to your family, friends, coworkers, and yourself every day you will be amazed at the results.

What Now?

I hope you enjoyed reading, this, my very first book, as much as I enjoyed writing it! But this is only the tip of the iceberg . . . *there is so much more to learn!*

I cover some of this in the final video at the link below. I hope you see the end of this book as the beginning to a new way of life. If you want to learn more about our Power of Positive Reinforcement DVD, webinars, and workshops, as well as our Smartcard Reinforcement System ™ please visit us on the web at www.powerofpositivereinforcement.com today!

I have a few closing thoughts in a final video
for you at the link below.
www.powerofpositivereinforcement.com

ABOUT THE AUTHOR

Bill Sims, Jr., is President of The Bill Sims Company, Inc. For nearly 30 years, Bill has created behavior-based recognition programs that have helped large and small firms to deliver positive reinforcement to inspire better performance from employees and increase bottom line profits.

Bill has delivered his "Green Beans & Ice Cream" leadership workshop and keynote speeches in Europe, the Middle East, most of the USA, Australia and many parts of Africa.

This book is based on these sessions and his experience having built more than 1,000 positive reinforcement systems programs at firms including Dupont, Siemens VDO, Coca-Cola, and Disney, to name a few.

To learn more visit us at www.powerofpositivereinforcement.com

PR+ Leadership...One Scoop At A Time

I'm delighted that you have taken the time to explore my ideas for positive reinforcement and behavior change!

I hope that this small keepsake will help you remember the power of positive reinforcement. Before you know it, you will be dishing out scoops of positive feedback to others every single day. You see, this little tool is not only cute, it is powerful. It will help you change yourself, and master the power of positive reinforcement.

Start every day with all the ice cream cones lying on your desk, or in your pocket. Make it a goal to say something positive to at least three people every day (your kids, your spouse, your boss, your coworkers, and yes, even yourself!). Tell them what they did, and why that mattered to you. It's that simple.

Why not start right now with someone who made a difference to you?

Every time you positively reinforce someone, reward yourself and put one ice cream cone in the base. Don't go to bed until all three cones are back in their place.

Have fun!